To McKenzie,

You'll Do Anything For The One You Love The Most

The Lawkeeper, Lamb, Lion!

Chuck Beckler
12/11/14

CHUCK BECKLER

BE THOU MY VISION O' LORD OF MY HEART,
NAUGHT BE ALL ELSE TO ME SAVE THAT THOU ART.

DEDICATION

To Linda, my wife, for faithfully walking hand-in-hand with me on the loving, yet mysterious path of Divine Providence. Thanks for traveling, thinking and teaching with me the transforming story of the gospel. "You're Still the One" because "Never My Love".

To Jonathan & Becky, Matthew & Tiffany, our sons and their wives. Thanks for loving and cheering us on!

To Travis, our grandson, whose courage and celebration of life is an example to us all.

We're a family of God's Sovereign Grace and I'm forever grateful.

IT IS NEEDFUL TO AROUSE THE FAITHFUL
OTHERWISE TORPOR WILL CREEP IN THE FLESH.
JOHN CALVIN

ACKNOWLEDGMENTS

I am thankful for so many of you. To my parents, Mark and Jodie Beckler, for being the first to teach me the name Jesus; to those family and friends who believed in me and have given good words to press on; to Mom and Leanne Beutler, you've both been so kind; to Andy and Ella Lindvall for mentoring Linda and me patiently, also to Ella for your edit; to the True Direction family all over the place; to the "old dead guys," I'm grateful and we'll talk; to the wives of our TD board members, thanks for sharing your guys and your vision for the gospel; and finally to the edit and design team that wrapped it up, Dan Cox, Reg Hamilton, Ron Kirkeeng, and Jim Kohl. Thanks for making sense of my grammatical train wreck. Thanks for helping me stay on course doctrinally. Thanks for your uniquely creative personalities. Thanks for your time and vision for the gospel. I'm undeserving of your friendship. Thank you.

SPECIAL THANKS

Galen & Linda Ackerman
Bill & Laurel Cade
Tamra Coughlin
Jim & Jackie Kohl
Joe & Dianne Pannegasser
Steve & Mandy Reiff
Robert Schuman
Thrivent For Lutherans

CONTENTS

PROLOGUE: WHY?

We all like to begin well in anything we do and not give up in the process. We've been taught from pre-school to begin and finish a job with excellence. And with that in mind, I wanted this book to both begin and end well. How I have done will be left for you the reader to determine. So, please begin and finish the book and let me know what you think. Remember to extend some mercy to me since it is my first effort.

I mentioned to somebody that I was writing a book and he asked me, "Why?" It was a good question and I'm thinking that's a great place to begin. The simple and brief response is, "I was asked to write a book." It really didn't come from me initially. I didn't have an epiphany, a dream or a strange vision. But what I did have was a mass of people telling me over thirty years of speaking to write a book.

I had developed a series of talks at different venues over the years, and people really seemed to enjoy them. At different speaking dates I would get requests for a tape, video, DVD, or a book. The encouragement from people would come into my head and exit rapidly. But the push to put this series into print kept coming like a relentless swarm of bees. Setting it all aside, I worked on developing new material.

The years have flown by and I've been blessed with loving mentors and board members for True Direction Ministries. They have been loving individuals of all kinds who have given much physical and mental time along with their kind financial support. The current board is a unique mix of guys and I'm thankful for all of them. At one of our meetings it was brought to the table for discussion that, "Chuck should write a book." The bees were buzzing. I told them I'd pray on it. I did, and it was the first time that I sensed, maybe I should write it. So, after praying and seeking God's direction in all of this, I agreed to accept their challenge and the journey began. For those of you who are *Lord of the Rings* freaks, I felt like I could shout along with Bilbo Baggins, "I'm going on an adventure." I can relate to the small, large hairy-footed Hobbits. The adventure began and I wrote a book, never really imagining I could have anything of real significance to do in this world seemingly loaded with orcs and goblins.

But the truth is that before the foundations of the world were formed, God had plans for my life. He uses all of His precious saints for His glory in some mysterious manner. I never imagined all of the privileges He would extend to me in His mercy and grace. He'd bring me into this world using the earthly vehicles of my Mom and Dad, whom He would save. They would take me to Sunday School while I was still in my mother's womb. I faithfully attended Awana Clubs and weekly Christian Service Brigade meetings where I would win candy bars. Every summer it was Bible Memory Association camp Michigan. I'd memorize Bible verses all year long attend a free week of camp and become the favorite o. all the cabin counselors. The counselors may not have said that I was their favorite, but I promise you that they knew my name. I was the master of catching and releasing gophers and frogs into the girls' cabins at night. I can still remember the screams in the cabins—it was awesome! As a result of my little escapades I learned to scrub toilets until they'd shine brilliantly. We had "Family Altar" in our home every night and that's where I first met John Bunyan and his pilgrim called "Christian." If there was ever a kid that had the Word of God taught to him in large doses, it was me. (I also had some large portions of liver that were apparently good for me, but most of those portions ended up in my little pockets!) I had great times in those early days of my youth, it was a blast! But I also think about all the people I almost drove to madness. In fact, it's during those reflective moments that I wish I could say to them these words: "I'm sorry for being a punk. Thank you for teaching me God's Word with great love."

I made an emotional decision as a little boy to ask Jesus into my heart, and that's all it was—an emotional decision. I've also come to this conclusion as I've wrestled doctrinally through the years with this issue: it really wasn't God's grace at work in my life. It was only an emotional decision made by a scared little boy. Please think about that and don't tune me out. I'm convinced that when any five year old is presented with either the joy of heaven or the tortures of eternal punishment in a place called hell, he or she will choose heaven every time. I'm not blaming anybody for anything they did during my childhood. But I am asking you to think with me carefully

...ut these issues. Perhaps a part of my decision was a ...sponse to please Mommy and Daddy, to do what they ...anted me to do.

At this moment I'm asking the parents who are reading this to take a little time to process what I'm saying. We love our children with all of our hearts and want each of them to spend eternity in heaven. But that needs to be a result of God's loving grace in their lives, and we need to trust Him and His plans. Through my early teen years and into college there was no Biblical fruit or expressions of God's grace in my life, and yet I had said "the prayer." Yep, I went to church and prayed. I even hung out at youth group and attended Youth for Christ meetings at Moody Church. (There were girls all over the place at those meetings). It seemed like I went to every church event a teenager could attend and have some fun. But the fruit of the Spirit wasn't to be found any place in my daily life. There was a contradiction in my life. I'd even been baptized and shared my testimony many times in different church settings. My life was a sinful mess on a regular basis. But in a "safe" environment where I wouldn't be publically identified with Jesus, I'd do the Christian stuff. I was deceived and I didn't know it or really even think about my behavior as a problem. I had "asked Jesus into my heart" and that covered all of the sin patterns in my life. But, my destination was hell, and I wasn't aware of that painful eternal surprise waiting for me at any moment while I lived a life mocking God. I really hope you're connecting the dots of my story with my concerns about, "saying the prayer," or "asking Jesus into your heart." That kind of thinking in the church is one of the key motivations for taking the challenge to write this book.

But then I was mercifully surprised by God and His amazing grace in my early twenties. My wife, Linda, and I had been married for quite some time and God had given us a little dude to whom I would sing and play my guitar. I had been singing in a rock band several nights a week all over the Midwest and I lived a rather selfish life which caused everyone around me undeserved pain. It was in the spring months of the year when God rescued me from His wrath of eternal punishment. He gave instantaneous spiritual sight to a spiritually blind man. He granted me the ability to understand my helpless position under the curse of the law. It was at that helpless and terrifying moment in His perfect plan for my life that I saw Jesus. No, I didn't have a vision or a weird out of body experience. The Holy Spirit regenerated me and I was able to see Jesus as the much needed Savior of my life. If you've ever read the story of the prodigal son in Luke 15, that was me. I repented and confessed my sin and He forgave me.

My conversion and living relationship with Christ was not a result of man's doing, but God's. God also allowed me to go to my earthly father and repent and restore our relationship. Of course my mom was also involved in that process of healing relationships in our family. Like the apostle Paul, God's love, mercy and grace had smacked me upside the head and had given me a new heart. Regenerated, born again and changed by grace, the fruit of the Holy Spirit was now becoming evident in my life. God had grown within my heart new appetites, attitudes and actions. I was a new creation in Christ and as long as He allows me, I'll proclaim His mighty and majestic works to everyone possible.

In November of 1983, I left my sales position which I really enjoyed. God had called me out and into full-time vocational ministry as a youth pastor. It's been an incredible journey with all of the twists and turns that you might expect. I've heard it said that ministry and the Christian life is a battle, not a dream. The battle has been worth it all and I'd choose it every time even in light of all the struggles Linda and I have gone through within the mystery of Providence. I'm still amazed at the un-

STRATEGY WITHOUT CHARACTER IS WORTHLESS.

believable privileges God has given to both of us. From a youth pastor to itinerate speaker and discipleship trainer with Son Life Ministries speaking at conferences all over North America, I stand amazed. I'm amazed that God graciously rescued me and would use me to speak, and now write, to so many. I love the privilege and tread cautiously as I go and teach *His* Word and not mine.

As I reflect on my past life, I'm convinced that there are many people within the church who are still deceived like I was in my youth. So I began years ago to develop talks and sermons that would hopefully challenge people of all ages to think and evaluate their relationship with Jesus. As I mentioned earlier in this introduction, one of the talks I'd been giving kept getting requested. I actually had a friend tell me, "I think it's anointed." I'm not exactly sure what he meant by that within his theological grid work, but it was a nice compliment. And the talk that was constantly asked for is now in your hands to read.

I'm radically passionate about Christ's words in the Bible, especially those related directly to discipleship. I love the development of discipleship strategy and philosophy of ministry. But that is not what this book is about. This book is about "The Character of a True Disciple of Christ." The question that you might be asking is, "Which is more important—discipleship strategy or character development?" Can you guess? Let me take a moment here to throw out some thoughts for you to consider on this issue. I think strategy development has taken the lead in the church today. But, strategy without character is worthless. Go on and dive into the book and you'll see what I mean.

There's great confusion and conflict within the church today over discipleship strategy and character. These two issues directly relate to an incorrect understanding and communication of the gospel, as expressed in such things as "asking Jesus into your heart" or "praying the sinner's prayer." These are human words and thoughts which do not accurately teach the Biblical truth of the gospel. I'm asking you to think about that. A great preacher from several years ago, A.W. Tozer, had the same concerns and said,

> *"Jesus Christ has today almost no authority at all among the groups that call themselves by His name. The present position of Christ in the gospel churches may be likened to that of a king in a limited, constitutional monarchy. The king in such a country is no more than a traditional rallying point, a pleasant symbol of unity and loyalty much like a flag or a national anthem. He is lauded, feted and supported, but his real authority is small. Nominally he is head*

over all, but in every crisis someone else makes decisions."

These are very strong words from an old dead guy, but I think he nails it.

We all struggle with the authority of anyone in our lives telling us how to live. The authority problem begins for each of us at conception and continues until we die. Until the day we die we want to do it our way! Didn't someone sing a song about that? I have moments of internal raging battle with authority that still baffles my brain and scares me. This book attacks that difficult human battle of "who's the boss?"—who has the real authority in your life? I know, let's not talk about the boss, but as Christians we have no choice. Jesus has expressed clear demands for those who will follow Him. He is the boss. I thank God every day that He is not a bullish tyrant, but my loving Father.

In summary, this book is about exposing the deception and confusion of the words "asking Jesus into your heart," or "I've said the prayer." It's also about Biblical commitment, character and following hard after Christ throughout your entire life. It's about loving Him because He first loved us! I hope you'll be encouraged and challenged to think Biblically about the words of Jesus. My words are not inspired by God—I'm very aware of my weak human mind and physical frailties. I'm not infallible or inerrant, but His Word is. My prayer is that you will examine His words carefully, taking great care for your soul's well-being. Malachi 2:7 says, "For the lips of a priest should guard knowledge and people should seek instruction from his mouth, for he is the messenger of the Lord of Hosts." I pray that, as a type of messenger from the Lord, I have honored those words for my soul's well-being, as well as yours. So please read on. Think, laugh, cry, get angry if you must and wrestle with Jesus' words, because I know they'll change your life now and for eternity.

SOLI DEO GLORIA!

.

1
THE BOWLING ALLEY

Several years ago, I was asked to speak at a student ministry activity in Michigan. I said yes and off I went to the land of lakes and camps. The event was called a lock-in and it was held at a bowling alley. The idea was to spend the entire night bowling with high school students. My responsibility was to talk about Jesus and stay alive. I'm serious! You dare not fall asleep, or you become prey for the pranksters. I've seen students bowl with each other, and frankly I wasn't up for becoming a giant human bowling ball. It always amazes me that we spend so much money doing all kinds of crazy activities within the body of Christ, but they do create a great environment to connect with students. They love it! That's the way I've lived for many years traveling around the country speaking at all kinds of youth and family events, and this was one of those crazy fun times.

While I was watching students toss one another down the lanes of the bowling alley, I became aware that two girls were heading my way, sobbing and slobbering all over one another. I thought for a moment and decided that they probably had a boyfriend problem, and at three o'clock in the morning, I wasn't ready to deal with it. So I prayed, "God, grant me wisdom to give great Biblical counsel to these two who seem to be so miserable in the middle of the early morning. Please help me not to be too sarcastic, but love them with your love." God responded. At least, I thought He was responding to me with this incredible loving counsel: "Tell the girls if it's a boyfriend problem, they should pray and consider this heavenly strategy. First, find one of the largest bowling balls in the alley. Second, look the young man in his eyes to get his attention and then drop the bowling ball on his toes." You're probably thinking that's not the best counsel to give girls at 3:00am. I plead exhaustion and delirium. It was an all-nighter and I was fried. But you're right—what was I thinking?

As the girls came closer to me I realized there was a major problem. They were sobbing and slobbering all over one another and chewing on each other's hair—that's serious. They were just a few feet from me and I had to respond to them quickly. I looked at both of them, and trying to be as compassionate as I could, I asked, "Girls, what's up? What's wrong? Why are you both so upset?" They began to jump up and down hugging each other over and over while almost falling on the floor and me. Their response startled me, and I really didn't know what to say. They said, "We're not upset. We're excited! We're happy!" I asked, "Excited and happy about what?" They cried even louder!

At that point, I realized that girls can cry upset or cry excited. Forgive me, but I had two sons, so I didn't quite get it. There have been times when I've been speaking and some young ladies take issue with me about why girls cry. My response is, "Be thankful you don't cry like boys; they just go blah, blah" and I ease my way out of the situation. Finally, I did blurt out in frustration, "So girls really do cry about almost anything?" That was not the best thing to say at that moment. They both looked at me with fire in their eyes and said, "We have something to tell you and it's very, very important." Curiosity had the best of me. What could make two girls so wired and crazy at three in the morning, if not death or a boyfriend crisis? They both said almost simultaneously, "We just asked Jesus into our hearts." One girl said to me, "Not me, but her." I've heard that said many times during thirty years of ministry. My mind went into a deep freeze as I quickly tried to think of some response that would be encouraging and not too offensive.

I must confess that I was doubting what took place in the life of this girl. Be patient with me here. I want all people to come to saving faith in Christ, but the worst thing that could happen to anyone is human manipulation into a false conversion. I didn't want that for this girl. They were both still crying, hugging, slobbering on each other and me. For a moment I thought, "Well LORD, if they're saved, take them both to heaven now before they drown me in their slobbering." I didn't really mean that, but we all have strange thoughts at times. Heaven's cool, right? They hadn't moved. They stood there with asking eyes waiting for the speaker who supposedly had shared the gospel to celebrate with them, or at least give a word of advice.

I finally pulled myself together and gathered my

thoughts. It was time to give them an explanation of soteriology. That is, what God does to save us. It is the amazing doctrine of salvation and all the trimmings. I felt quite proud of myself that I could remember anything at 3:00am. When I finished with my little presentation, the girls looked at me like I had just blown their minds. I was still feeling pretty good about my doctrinal discourse that covered everything from regeneration to propitiation to justification to sanctification to the preservation of the saints and even a touch of eschatology. I had been so caught up in my presentation about God's works of grace, that I missed the change of their facial expressions. Their faces now exhibited startled, stunned looks of minds on overload, and I had missed it. I really had a sincere desire in my heart to help these two girls understand the seriousness of the gospel message. I ended with this, "Girls, isn't it incredible what God did for us? He sent His Son to do what Adam failed to do— keep the law. Jesus is the Lamb who took the wrath of His Father—hell—and made peace for those who, by faith, believe in His works—not theirs. He rose from the grave conquering death and the devil, proving that He is the Son of God. Jesus stepped out of heaven and down to this earth He created in order to save those who were under the curse of the law. Girls, Jesus is the Savior, Hero, Rescuer, Peacemaker." I quoted Scripture, and told them all about God's love, mercy and grace. I also wanted to make sure they understood God's forgiveness, and what a beautiful gift that is for those who repent and believe in Christ. Man, I was having a moment of my own!

You can't help getting wired after running through all God has done for you. It gets emotional, you know? I said, "So, ladies, what do you think about all I've said?" They said, "That's all cool! But we're just so excited that we'll live together in heaven forever!" With that, they began jumping up and down and spinning around together. Not wanting to be a party pooper, I prayed again and hesitated to speak. I finally spoke up and asked them this question, "What about living for Jesus now? Would you like to know what He wants from us while we live on this earth until heaven? You know, what a disciple of Jesus should act like?" They both simultaneously and enthusiastically shouted, "YES." So I opened my Bible to Luke chapter 14 and asked them to read verses 25-33. They took it and ran off. I thought for a moment, "I'll never see my Bible again." I had this horrible thought I'd see it making its way down one of the lanes. It probably wouldn't be malicious, but when it comes to student ministries, things happen. Well, they were gone and I went back to watching seniors use sleepy ninth-graders as bowling balls. I told you... it's youth ministry and I've seen goofier things take place, from eating live spiders and dead fish to much, much more. Someday I might write a book about all that kind of stuff. It could have the makings of a best seller.

After some time had gone by, during the wee hours of the morning I'd forgotten about the girls and my Bible. Suddenly, there they were with my Bible in hand and bewildered looks on their faces. They wanted to talk, and I mean talk! They had serious questions about the meaning of Jesus' words in the text I'd given them to read. Have you read Luke 14:25-33? It really is a powerful, mind-boggling passage. It's one where you say to yourself, "I'll think about it later." Desperately I prayed, "Lord help me!" Before I could gather my

SHE LOOKED AT ME AS IF I WERE A TRAITOR...RUINING EVERYTHING SHE HAD DONE.

thoughts, they exploded with their concerns. The girl who said she had prayed the prayer asking Jesus into her heart began. "I don't understand what Jesus is saying here, what He is saying really scares me." She continued with tears beginning to build again in her eyes and shouting, "I can't hate my parents!" "No, no" I said, "not hate them, but less devotion to them. His words and will for your life are to be more important than anyone, including mother and father or boyfriend."

There seemed to be a change in her body language and facial expression. She looked angry and said, "That wasn't in the prayer." With frustration building in her she asked, "And what about this taking up your cross?" Carefully, with as much compassion as I could express, I said, "Yes, He wants us to be willing to die for Him, if that's what He has planned for us. Blood for blood." Her look was one of devastation and confusion. Once again she cried out, "That wasn't in the prayer." My heart was breaking for her. Had she become another victim of our evangelical blundering of the gospel? Her friend stood stunned and speechless. She looked at me as if I were a traitor, heretic or at least an evil monster ruining everything she had done. She asked one more question of me, "He wants all my possessions, all, all, everything?" What was I supposed to say? "Well, Jesus didn't really mean what He said. What He really meant to say was something like this, 'If you're interested in giving them up, we can make a deal.'"

It's always been incredible to me how we love to tell others what Jesus is trying to tell them—how we love to fix up what He's trying to communicate. She shook my Bible and said, "None of it; none of it was in the prayer. I prayed to go to heaven with my friend, not have my whole life changed and rearranged, that's not what I asked for!" I responded as gently as I could and said to her, "But that's the deal." I reminded her that it's a blood for blood relationship that involves a supernatural change of life. It's God's Spirit working in us, giving us new attitudes and appetites. Jesus came to save His people from their sins, transforming them into His image, with His goals becoming their goals, and living lives that do not conform to, nor are controlled by, the thinking of this world. Before I could go on explaining, sadly, the girl who said she had prayed the prayer said to me, "If that's what Jesus wants, I want no part of it!" Frustrated, she threw my Bible at me and they bolted. I stood there stunned and disappointed. Perhaps flabbergasted would be a better description of how I felt at the moment.

They were gone and my heart was grieved. What happened? I prayed and begged God to have mercy on them both. I also asked the Holy Spirit to please fix anything that I might have messed up. As I turned this encounter with the girls over and over In my mind, exhaustion was rapidly setting in. I was tired, both emotionally and physically. Suddenly, there was a tap on my shoulder. I thought, "They're here. They've come back and want to talk." But when I lifted my head I wasn't looking at the girls. Rather, it was the face of a frustrated youth pastor. He asked, "Beckler, what are you doing? Two of our girls said you completely confused them. What in the world did you say to them?" The lock-in was just about over and I was spent in body and soul. I prayed silently, "Lord help me to lovingly and accurately explain." I looked right into his eyes and said, "I walked them back through the gospel. I explained His love, mercy and grace the best that I could. I told them all Jesus had done. I was careful. Then I asked them if they wanted to know what He expects from His followers. I only told them what Jesus did and would have said if He were here."

I was never asked to speak for that specific group again. My brain aches sometimes as I think about that night long ago in a bowling alley. My heart's desire was never to hurt those girls. They are God's creations and I don't want to offend Him! I wanted them to understand the true gospel and its saving power. I wanted to meet them in heaven someday and celebrate with them God's riches for His children. I'm still praying for that to happen. The mysteries of God are way, way beyond me. His wisdom is perfect, and mine is not, but I can still have loving concerns, right? These concerns have been stirring in my heart and mind for years. These concerns have come as a result of studying God's Word and interacting with thousands of people. These concerns are a result of my own childhood experiences.

The concern that tops my list is terrifying and heart-wrenching: people of all ages being manipulated into emotional, false conversions! It is people thinking they are saved, when they are not. How eternally tragic. I've seen it, and I'm committed to exposing the problem. Perhaps at one point early in my ministry I was guilty of a type of manipulation. God have mercy! I tremble to think that the girls at the bowling alley are just two out of the many that are misled, perhaps even by those with pure motives. They may have pure motives, but they are misinformed about the gospel and its power. There is a Divine punch of power to the gospel. New creations are made! Luke 14 has a three-punch combination knockout blow, describing for us what new creations should look like, if they've been lovingly punched by God's grace. Saul, the killer of Christians, was punched off his horse by God's love and he became Paul, the loving messenger of the gospel. He was a changed man. Life transformation is an essential part of the gospel! Read on and keep thinking, but please don't throw your Bible at me. I'll never catch it.

2
THE PUNCH

The purpose of this chapter is to take a closer look at Luke 14:25-33, hopefully without messing it up. I mentioned in chapter one that we love to try to fix or explain Jesus' teaching—especially the tough words from Him. My desire is not to "fix" anything about the Son of God. That doesn't even make sense! I just want us to go slowly through the text and cautiously meditate upon it. As we evaluate it, I pray that the Holy Spirit will instruct you in the powerful meaning of His words.

If I were speaking to you at a conference, I would begin this session by saying something like this: "The two girls in the bowling alley got punched by Jesus right in the face." When I say this, the looks on the faces of the audience are amazing. There are expressions that range from confusion to anger to skepticism to, "You're not telling the truth." I've actually had people say, "Chuck, c'mon man, Jesus wouldn't hit anyone. He's a lover, not a fighter." My response in my mind and sometimes audibly is, "I'm glad He's both." I don't know why we can't see Jesus for who He is. The Gospels give us exact word pictures of His character and ministry. I know I'll miss something about Him that you'll remember, but consider this description of Jesus: He was a thinker, confronter, warrior, lover, fighter, compassionate caregiver, servant, prayer, protector, weeper, miracle worker, demon caster, preacher, teacher, and God in the flesh who sometimes packed a spiritual punch that knocked crowds off their feet and scared them to death!

I've felt that punch at times, and so have you if you've been hanging around Jesus for a while. The girls at the bowling alley felt it and it knocked them off their feet and unraveled their thinking. You may not want to think about this, but maybe you need some unraveling in your life. The Bible is timeless. It doesn't evolve with our evangelical changes. It has no place for morphs that have gradually watered down the presentation of the gospel message, leaving us with a pragmatic gospel that relies on man's methods instead of God's power alone. The challenge from Jesus is the same today as it was two thousand years ago. It is a blood for blood deal, and it's all about love. It's all about how His love changes us and motivates us to live for Him with an uncompromising passion. So please read on and think about it until it hurts, because in the hurting there's healing.

Think about it. How could a punch from God not heal your soul? Some old French guy said something like this, "If you make people think they're thinking, they'll love you. But if you really make them think, they might hate you." I don't want you to hate me. But I do want you to think because I care about your eternal destiny. When I was a little boy, if someone had said, "Go sit over there and think about what I just said to you. It's for your own good" the last thing I wanted to do was go sit and think. I just wanted to play! The enemy doesn't want thinking, just playing. But we need to think so that the playing becomes more fun! So here we go. And by the way, I use the new authorized version of the Bible called the English Standard Version. If you don't have this version, get it!

Luke 14:25-33 English Standard Version (ESV)

25 Now great crowds accompanied him, and he turned and said to them, 26 "If anyone comes to me and does not hate his own father and mother and wife and children and brothers and sisters, yes, and even his own life, he cannot be my disciple. 27 Whoever does not bear his own cross and come after me cannot be my disciple. 28 For which of you, desiring to build a tower, does not first sit down and count the cost, whether he has enough to complete it? 29 Otherwise, when he has laid a foundation and is not able to finish, all who see it begin to mock him, 30 saying, 'This man began to build and was not able to finish.' 31 Or what king, going out to encounter another king in war, will not sit down first and deliberate whether he is able with ten thousand to meet him who comes against him with twenty thousand? 32 And if not, while the other is yet a great way off, he sends a delegation and asks for terms of peace. 33 So therefore, any one of you who does not renounce all that he has cannot be my disciple.

PUNCH, PUNCH and PUNCH! Did you hear and feel it? The crowd had to be stunned and staggered. The language in the original is overwhelmingly powerful.

When it says, "He turned and said to them," it was as if He had broken all their noses! I've had my nose broken six times; it hurts! I have to believe the crowd was thinking at that moment, "Where's the love?" Why had the gentle teacher who fed them and healed them just hurt them? Or, maybe they thought, "He can't be serious about all of this. It sounds just like the Pharisees—more legalistic demands. Another rabbi teaching more things to do, more works to be at peace with God." If that was they were thinking, they were dead wrong, like so many others who don't listen carefully to Him. Perhaps they didn't hear Him correctly because they were too preoccupied with what He would do next. They loved the healings and the food from His fingertips. Did they follow Him only to get? Were they just takers? These words from His lips were demanding, just too demanding for them to process. They were right. The words are extremely demanding for all of us. If we're honest with ourselves about the text, it affects us the same way it did the crowd. It hurts, and challenges our thinking.

I was speaking at a camp and teaching this passage. When I finished and was heading back to my cabin in the woods to reflect and pray for the group, I heard yelling coming from behind me. A shot of fear raced through my body and my heart pounded. I turned around to see what was up, hoping that I wouldn't get a pie or shaving cream in the face or worse. The yelling was coming from a group of cabin counselors. I began to figure out what they were saying and it was worse than a pie in the face. I heard things like heretic, works salvationist, legalist, false teacher and more. I was looking for the ropes that would be used to tie me up. When they caught up and confronted me, it was almost frightening. They said, "Chuck you taught the text all wrong. You taught the students they we're saved by works and not by faith." I really didn't want a theological or doctrinal brawl in the woods. Besides, they were all bigger than me and it just wasn't right. I asked if we could speak at another time. Their response was, "No, we'll fix your mess with the students." They disappeared into the dark of the night and I stood wondering.

That wasn't the first time—or last time—something like that had happened to me when I taught that passage. Luke 14 rocks us, jolts us. It's not a pat on the back or a nice shoulder rub. It goes straight to the heart and squeezes hard. It forces us to catch our breath or at least try to figure out a way to soften the blow. I've taught this passage hundreds of times and have been encouraged and confronted about it more than any other text I've taught. Why? What causes so much emotional, personal and sometimes almost violent reaction? It's the demands of Jesus! His three-punch combination! He makes it very clear that if we're going to call ourselves His disciples, there are certain demands that must be met.

The term "disciples" in the text is synonymous with the title "Christian" and these demands must be, as John MacArthur says, "if not the perfection of our lives then they must be the direction of our lives." Please take a moment to reflect upon that. The three demands are very, very personal. They cause us to take a scary look at our Christian lives, performing a type of spiritual surgery. They expose us to ourselves and that's the job of the text and the Holy Spirit. So climb up on the operating table and ask God's Spirit to please go to work. Jesus said to His disciples, "If you love Me, you will keep My commandments." Luke 14 is all about love, commands and demands. Read on!

The first demand Jesus challenges the crowd with involves *people*—close and important relationships. He lists almost all the earthly relationships you can think of. Sometimes when I speak to students they'll say, "Chuck, it doesn't say boyfriend or girlfriend or friends in general, just family, right?" Man, we're good, aren't we? When I get asked that question I always know someone's dating somebody they shouldn't be dating. Wow! That's a whole other issue, maybe one for another book. I'm convinced the first demand made by Jesus is crystal clear for all of us. Here it is again. Please read it slowly. We are to have no other person or persons directing our lives. He is the supreme and ultimate authority, boss, trainer, coach, friend in our lives. Did I miss one? Yep, not even ourselves. We've been bought with a precious price that cost Him more than we'll ever understand. He owns us! Therefore, no musician, actor, celebrity, counselor, magazine—anything or anyone else—deserves our devotion and love like Jesus does. All decisions must meet with His approval. It makes so much sense! There will never be anyone who will love us like Him. No one but Him knows what's best for our lives! So, why do we continue to argue with the best? What's wrong with our brains? What's wrong with mine? Don't ask me or anyone who knows me—it's too scary. Let's face the fact that we love being the boss. The consequences of that fact can be devastating, if not

> ## WE ARE TO HAVE NO OTHER PERSON DIRECTING OUR LIVES.

fatal.

When I was a youth pastor, there was a girl in our ministry that simply rocked for Jesus. She studied God's Word and brought more students to our meetings than any other student. At one of our regular meetings a good looking athlete showed up. I'm not making fun of the girls in our group, but they all drooled. I mean drooled! The girls couldn't help themselves, he was a Chick Magneto. I realized there was trouble lurking because he wasn't a believer and I had to protect our ladies. In 2 Corinthians 6:14, God's Word makes it absolutely clear that, as believers, we're not to be joined together in an intimate relationship with non-believers. We carefully warned the girls to stay away from the young man who continued to attend the meetings. I firmly believe that in evangelism, girls should pursue girls and guys should pursue guys. This pattern of evangelism lines up with Biblical truth. I know by experience that by breaking God's pattern in this area could be a matter of life and death. If you're a parent, what pattern are you cultivating in your children?

Our guys were commissioned to take the gospel to this kid. His home-life was a mess and he needed Christ. Well, to make a long story short, that rockin' girl for Jesus said, "I'll go after him. It's not a problem for me." We can really deceive ourselves. Jeremiah 17:9 says, "The heart is deceitful above all things and desperately sick; who can understand it?" It was a great mistake for her to put this guy above Jesus and the Word of God. She broke the pattern and willingly indulged herself in sin. The consequences of her sin resulted in great pain for her and everyone else close to the situation. Whenever we elevate another person above Christ and make them the supreme person in our life and the object of our love which only He deserves, we sin. We actively ignore His demand and bring His discipline into our life. Or, if the pattern persists in our life, we prove we are not truly a disciple of His.

I'm really concerned about all of us understanding Jesus' demands. This first demand of having no person above Him in our lives must constantly be evaluated. Our love for Christ should be the motivation to put people in their proper place. I believe Jesus dealt with people and relationships first because people have a powerful influence over us. We watch, listen and then act like those we admire. When I was younger it went from Davy Crockett to The Beatles to many more. I wore a coonskin cap and I could sing like Paul or John. In a way, they had my attention and love. Even after God rescued me, there have been people I have admired too much. For a while, I thought I could be a Puritan or some great evangelist from the past. It wasn't bad to read and study their lives and learn from them. It becomes bad when I seek their counsel for life before the One I say I love the most. God has given us all kinds of relationships to cherish in this life. Parents, children, brothers, sisters, aunts, uncles, cousins, friends, neighbors and so on, and they are all to be enjoyed in their proper place. But there is not one of them that should ever take the place of Jesus—not for a moment!

The second demand of Jesus' three-punch combination might be even more powerful and problematic for us than the first. This demand is summed up in the unpopular, misunderstood and misused word, "persecution." I was speaking at a youth conference on the east coast. After one of the evening sessions, I was in the cafeteria calling Linda, my wife. While we were talking, the door flew open and in burst a mass of young guys with their leaders. I thought for a moment I was in the midst of a simulated S.W.A.T. raid. They ripped the phone out of my hand as I tried to yell to Linda that I would be back—I hoped. Then they proceeded to hang me on a hook up in the air. I hung there dangling like a wall decoration of some sort. They burst into laughter and fled from the scene of their loving, good intentioned crime. I hung there in silence for a moment and then thought, "How will I get down from here?" I wiggled, jerked and yelled for help while Linda was wondering what had happened to me. I thought for a minute and came to this conclusion: it was persecution. I was being persecuted for the sake of the gospel. It wasn't some form of Roman torture, but I had been hung on a hook, perhaps never to be heard from again.

Some of you are saying right now, "You're messed up in your brain." Well, your assessment is probably accurate, but I've heard "carrying your cross" described in crazier terms: homework, housework, mothers-in-law, car trouble, bugs, weather. You name it and I've most likely heard it. I believe that perspective dishonors the text and the redemptive work of Christ. The text speaks of blood, torture, pain and death directly connecting you to your relationship with Jesus. This absolutely sounds like no fun at all. I love humor and really believe it's good for the body and soul. I've tried to find a way to soften the punch of the text, to lighten it up a bit. There have probably been times when I have done that, and perhaps that's when the message gets watered down and lost. The demand Jesus gives the crowd is persecution. If you investigate the word a little bit, it means to be treated with hostility for political or religious beliefs.

In Luke 14:27, Jesus gives His second demand and it punches right to the heart. Did you know that's how to really knock someone out or even kill them? A blow to the heart will suddenly stop it from beating. I think to a certain degree that's what Jesus had in mind for those who had been enjoying the benefits He offered them. It was a real crowd stunning, heart stopper! I'm sure people gasped and said to each other, "Did He say what I thought He said?" I believe He was communicating this truth: If you openly identify with Me—My Kingdom, My purposes and all that I AM as the Messiah, the only begotten Son of Yahweh, the Savior that was prophesied in the Old Testament not only for Israel, but for the entire

IF YOU OPENLY IDENTIFY WITH ME, IF YOU CONFESS THIS PUBLICALLY AND LIVE MY GOSPEL OUT PRACTICALLY AND RADICALLY IN YOUR LIVES, YOU WILL BE PERSECUTED BECAUSE OF ME IN SOME WAY, PERHAPS EVEN DEATH.

world—if you confess this publically and live My gospel out practically and radically in your lives, you will be persecuted because of Me in some way, perhaps even death. He was telling them He came to save people from the Father's wrath. He would substitute and sacrifice His life in a bloody mess. He would take hell for those who would repent and believe in Him. He would be the Peacemaker with His Holy Father who demanded a perfect sacrifice for the sinner under the curse of the law. He came to do it all and He would accomplish the Divine purposes, the task set before Him from eternity past. He would promise this and more to all who would repent and believe in Him as the only way to the Father. He promised that He came so they might live abundant, spiritually centered lives. He promised forgiveness and much more than any human being could ever comprehend. He would do all of this for those who would believe and follow according to His demands. But in return He would demand all of their loyalty, to the point of death, even on a cross.

Troubling, isn't it? Is it really possible in this day and age that Jesus would call us to this level of commitment? I've been told that it is Divine hyperbole of some sort. Jesus was just making some dramatic overstatements in order to get their attention. Jesus used it to make His point. I agree He used big, big statements, but it wasn't just a communication trick. It wasn't a crowd shocking, smoke machine moment of entertainment. He made His point and the crowd understood. They had seen the Romans butcher thousands on crosses. The road into Jerusalem had been lined with the naked, beaten, suffocating victims crying out for mercy. The victims would sometimes hang for weeks and die slowly while birds picked at their eyes and flesh. The crowd two thousand years ago understood that the cross meant a horrific death. In his commentary on Matthew 10, John MacArthur says this, "The cross symbolized the extremes of both excruciating pain and heartless cruelty; but above all it symbolized death. Only a few years before Jesus spoke those words, a zealot named Judas had gathered together a band of rebels to fight the Roman occupation forces. The insurrection was easily quelled, and in order to teach the Jews a lesson, the Roman general Varus ordered the crucifixion of over 2,000 Jews. Their crosses lined the roads of Galilee from one end to the other."

They remembered and I'm sure visualized in their mind's eye the picture that was so vivid to them of shame, humiliation, torture, pain and death. It wasn't representative of anything else. Jesus was clear. He wanted them to take up their own cross and follow closely after Him. G. Campbell Morgan, an old dead preacher guy, said this, "He wanted Battlers, Builders," those who would follow Him through all the days of their lives. Those who would sometimes fail with their faith, but would get up again and fight on, live on and love on. They would embrace the cross of Persecution because they love the One who kept the Law for them. They would be willing to bleed emotionally and physically because they love the One who is called the Lamb of God and bled for them. I can never hear it enough—the Savior who would take hell for them. They would follow hard trying to live a life of loving obedience, even when persecuted for living like their King, "The Lion of Judah."

Do you understand it a little more? It was love for love and blood for blood that Jesus demanded and the crowd was shocked and hushed. As a communicator, it was the perfect time for what He did next. In verses 28-32, He tells two stories to illustrate His demand and challenge the crowd to think. Evaluate His words carefully! He never uses emotional manipulation. He is the perfect teacher. He doesn't try to create a mood of response. Jesus, in all Divine sincerity says, "THINK"! It was approximately six months before He would cry out, "It is finished!" The feedings were over, the miracles almost done. He shouts out, "Think about what I'm demanding from those who will say they're My disciples." It was as if He used that little cliché we've all heard, "Think before you jump!" I've jumped way too often when I should have thought about making promises. What about you? He wanted good critical thinking from those in the crowd about making this commitment. He knows the heart of man and will not take advantage of them like so many had done.

I was speaking years ago at a youth conference and they wanted me to call for a response to the gospel. I asked if I could do it using the method I was comfortable with. I was given the green light and proceeded with caution. I called for a response and students stood up all over the room. I then proceeded to ask them, "Why?" Suddenly there was a mad rush to sit down again all over the room. I think they sat back down again because of this reason: in most situations, people are told why to stand, almost putting the words right in their mouths. I was asking them to tell all of us in their own words, why they were standing. I didn't want to put words in their mouths and play the part of the Holy Spirit. I wanted them to think and express for themselves their response to the gospel. Some people have told me, "They don't know what to say." My response is to say that I refuse to do for them what they need to do for themselves. It has to be from their own heart and mind in this eternal situation. I've tried to closely study Christ's style of ministry and how He called people to respond. Most, if not all of the time, He challenged individuals to process the information He'd given them. Think and then follow. And all of what we've been talking about is a mysterious work of God.

One of my favorite quotes is from a mentor who resides in heaven now. I didn't know him personally, but his writings have shaped my thinking *powerfully* over the years. When he was still in college he said, "He is no fool who gives what he cannot keep, to gain what he cannot lose." His name is Jim Elliot. You see, Jim understood. It's Blood for blood! A relationship with the living God and the incredible mysteries of eternity are worth more than anything this world has to offer. As a result of understanding all that Jesus had done for him, he embraced all three demands in Luke 14. Elliot and four others took the gospel to Ecuador, and the violent Waodani tribe mutilated and killed them. They were all speared over and over to the point of death. Were they perfect men? Were Jim Elliot, Ed McCully, Nate Saint, Roger Youderian and Pete Fleming all perfect in their daily lives? Absolutely not—no way. I've read excerpts from diaries and many books about their lives. But they were five young men who had thought about the demands of Christ in this text and in many others in God's Word. God had saved them by faith in the works of Christ alone and not theirs. They stood justified—not guilty before God's throne of Divine justice. And motivated by a love for their King, they went and gave their lives on the altar of sacrifice. They proved who they were—disciples, Christians, followers because they bore the cross, came after and followed.

Does Jesus call us all to this kind of end in life? For you and me, I don't know. But demand number two is real. It's Blood for blood, Love for love, Life for life—the real life of abundant living. Think about it. And by the way, that demand comes from Jesus, not from me. Every day of my life I have to deal with it just like you. The only way to avoid it is to ignore it! Be like so many others who just pass those tough words by or attribute them to Divine overstatements. I wonder if the crowd began to thin out. I wonder if people said, "I don't need this in my life, it's difficult enough!" I wonder if some parents said, "Children, cover your ears. The teacher has gone mad!" I wonder what it was like in that crowd, at that moment when no punches were pulled. Jesus didn't hold back; He gave the full blow. He punched with His Divine power.

In John 6:54, Jesus said, "Whoever feeds on my flesh and drinks my blood has eternal life, and I will raise him up on the last day." The theology and doctrine of that demand blew the crowd away. They grumbled and I'm sure they shook their heads and walked away. He looked at the twelve disciples, His intimate trainees, and asked them something like this, "What about you? Are you leaving too?" I know you want me to conclude the story in John, but I want you to read it for yourself. Go on and read the whole chapter. There are similarities in it to Luke 14. His teaching was so radical on occasions that people were bewildered. They exclaimed, "He teaches as one having authority and not like the Pharisees." At times He punched hard and people were rocked, emotions were unraveled and hearts trembled with fear. The cross will have that effect on us, especially if we're thinking about it in Jesus' terms. It demands blood! Martin Luther said, "He who is not a *crucianus* is not a *christianus*. He who does not bear his own cross is no Christian for he is not like his master." Think about that.

The third demand in Luke 14:25-33 is again pointed

right at our hearts, which makes it very personal. Jesus wraps up His challenge to the crowd rather abruptly. He ends it with what I call the stranglehold. Those three words alone take my breath away and bring back some scary memories. At the age of thirteen, I got myself into a fight after school. My sister, Diane, claims fighting was the pattern of my after-school life. It was my own after-school creative activity, kind of a sport. One day a classmate of mine got me in a stranglehold and I almost passed out. I will never forget that feeling of helplessness. He had me! With demand number three of Jesus' three-punch combination, He uses the stranglehold. It chokes off our airway and won't let us go! He goes after the darlings of our lives called possessions.

I remember training some church elders some time ago. I challenged them not to allow things of this world to control them. I challenged them to set an example for their congregation and to live sacrificially letting some of their "darlings" go. Suddenly I heard, "Be careful now, you're stepping on toes." I gently responded by saying, "I know, but here it is in God's Word." We all struggle with this teaching. This demand eats at us, strangles us and we'd rather not think about it too much. There have been many times when I've finished teaching on this demand and people almost rush the front where I'm standing and ask, "So what do you mean, am I supposed to give all, all my possessions to Jesus?" I know there's some kind of intense battle going on in that person's life with possessions and I really don't want to make it worse. So, I take a deep breath and say, "Let's read Jesus' words together again." We do, and it seems the internal battle intensifies. This punch stings! Jesus says, "Anyone who does not renounce *all*, CANNOT BE MY DISCIPLE!

Whatever you choose to call these, Jesus called them possessions. I'm not sure if we possess them, or they possess us. The word is a bit frightening if you really think about the meaning of it. We all know people who have fought and died for them. We store, hide and polish them and sometimes just get mesmerized over them, just as Golom treated "the precious", in Tolkien's *The Lord of the Rings*. He was consumed and controlled by power of the ring. Perhaps, in and of themselves, possessions are not inherently wrong. I really think it's you and me that have the problem. In my days as a youth pastor, Linda and I would occasionally have nursery duty. We love kids and didn't mind at all hanging out with the tiny dudes and dudettes. During those times I saw more brawls between the little creatures than you could imagine. One of them would grab a toy the other wanted and the intense battle for it was on. Sometimes there'd even be blood! And every once in a while a pacifier would be the focus of the fight. The warriors would grab it, stretch it and jerk it out of each other's mouths. It was an ancient form of ultimate fighting that was on display. With drool flowing everywhere the victor would come away with the prize in his or her mouth. I saw them whack one another with toys and beat each other with diapers.

Where did they learn this barbaric behavior? They were born with it, conceived in sin as King David explains to us in Psalm 51. It's called selfishness and all of us struggle with this ugly possessive behavior daily. We all want our binkies don't we? But the real problem sometimes is that we want everybody else's also. I'm going to deal with this demand in more detail later on in what I call the *apps* section of the book. It makes sense right—we're all into apps? (Someday, somebody reading this in the future will wonder, "What's an app?") The crowds in Luke 14 had been following and listening to Jesus. They loved the fast food, the healings and seeing the religious leaders of the day who were abusing them get smacked by this new Rabbi. But now this young teacher had also hurt them. He has punched them and demanded of them. The two previous demands were already more than they could take. I'm sure with this demand some in the crowd lost their appetite to eat. If they were to be His disciples (Christians) He had three powerful and non-negotiable demands that must be lived

HE ALONE MUST BE THE ULTIMATE OBJECT OF THEIR LOVE IF THEY WERE TO BE CALLED HIS DISCIPLES.

out in their lives daily. Their minds, their mouths, and the muscle of their bodies must be submitted to His authority.

The words of God in the flesh had put their minds on overload. I don't think anyone fell asleep during this sermon; it stirred up too much emotion. What do you think? Did the crowd break out into small group discussion? Seriously, what do you do at that moment? How in the world do you process or absorb those Divine thrusts to your heart? He must be the Supreme Person of their lives, directing all their thinking and actions. They must be willing to openly identify with Him and die for Him if necessary. And all their possessions were to be willingly used for His work. Nothing could control them in this life but Him. He alone must be the ultimate object of their love if they were to be called His disciples.

Doesn't this apply to all of us? The text has never changed. The words are just as powerful. The three-punch combination stops our hearts and creates fearful thoughts in our heads. We must deal with this honestly if we call ourselves Christians.

Linda and I were out in Washington state speaking at a youth camp. It is magnificent country in which to hang out. It's also the land of coffee—good coffee! We were driving off the camp grounds to get some of that wonderful stuff and have a little break in our busy day when I suddenly saw a man walking up the steep hill carrying a ball and chain. He was coming right toward us. I couldn't help myself, I just had to stop and find out who this guy was. My cautious wife was wisely asking me to be careful about all of this, and she was right. I guess any person attached to a ball and chain is a potential problem to our well-being. We stopped the car and the guy quickly came our way with his heavy looking outer wear. Before I could get out of the car door, he was at my window with a big smile. I was seriously hoping he wasn't going to drop that thing in my lap. We enjoyed a brief moment or two of casual conversation if that's possible with a man holding a ball and chain in his arms. Finally I asked him why and what and who he really was. His response stunned me! He told me that he was a school teacher on summer break. I rotated that thought quickly in my mind and came to the conclusion that he was misleading me. I asked him if the ball and chain was actually real and of course, heavy? He responded to me with a challenge to hold it in my own arms. I got out of the car very carefully watching his every move. The ball and chain that he'd been holding was very real and quite heavy. My crazy little brain was almost convinced for a short moment that he was a tricky escaped convict and I was in trouble. It was a very awkward moment as we stood there facing each other until he said to me, "I'm a Christian." Once again my mind was processing all kinds of weird information about this strange man with his questionable story. I then asked him to tell me what he was really doing.

Here is what he said to me: Every summer he walked across the entire state of Washington carrying his ball and chain so people would stop and ask him what he was doing. He would then proceed to share Christ with his roadside guests. I was amazed at what he'd just told me. He didn't take a summer job to earn more money but sacrificed all of that to bring the gospel to the lost. The desire to earn more in order to get more was not one of his life goals. We talked for a little while longer and then I needed to get back to camp to speak to the students. I wondered what the students would have thought had I brought him back to the camp with me. He taught me a great lesson that day about Jesus' third demand. I know you want me to share with you what I learned that day from one who was chained to Christ. Sorry, that is between my God and me. I want you to understand, I'm not copping out here. I was personally challenged to consider my struggle with my desire for more possessions. I hope that you'll contemplate my little adventure with that follower of Jesus and learn something for yourselves about the struggle with possessions in your life.

I want to conclude this chapter with some points to ponder. To really think about the Christianity Jesus has called us to, it takes constant reflection. I believe it's our responsibility as loving disciples of Jesus to learn, and evaluate our lives on a regular basis. The purpose is to stay on course and honor the King of Glory! Therefore, I'll give you a short list to help you stay on course. It's not necessarily a to-do list; it's more a think-about-it list. Most of us are trained within our education system to make the grade and get ahead. God has already performed and made the grade for those who are declared righteous. It was accomplished by the righteous-ness of His Son. So if that's you, you're not out to get a grade, get ahead or anything else. I've said that before, so I must really want that understood. So here we go! Read the list, think, ponder, contemplate and pray.

POINTS to PONDER

1. Salvation is by faith alone. You'll never earn it by trying to keep the demands of Luke 14.

2. These demands must be the direction of your life, if not the perfection of it.

3. Love is at the heart of these demands. It is the motivation of response.

4. The word "cannot" is used three times by Jesus. He is saying you don't have the right to say you are His disciple unless these demands are being worked out with love in your life.

5. There are many who say they have prayed the "sinner's prayer," but see this text as optional to the Christian. They are misled and are in serious danger of eternal punishment. Please pray and reconsider the words of Jesus in Luke 14.

O LORD OF LOVE AND LORD OF PAIN,
WHO, BY THY BITTER CROSS,
DOST TEACH US HOW TO MEASURE GAIN,
AND HOW TO MEASURE LOSS
WHOM, SEEING NOT, OUR HEARTS ADORE,
WE BRING OUR LOVE TO THEE;
AND WHERE THOU ART, LORD,
EVERMORE WOULD WE THY SERVANTS BE.
AMY CARMICHAEL

Amy Carmichael served for 55 years as a missionary at the Dohnavur Fellowship in India. If you don't know her, you need to become friends with this woman of faith.

THE ONLY PERSON WHO HAS THE RIGHT TO SAY
HE IS JUSTIFIED BY GRACE ALONE,
IS THE ONE WHO HAS LEFT ALL TO FOLLOW CHRIST.
DIETRICH BONHOEFFER

*Dietrich Bonhoeffer was a German pastor and author during
the years of Adolf Hitler's control of Germany. He stood
against the evils of Nazism and boldly proclaimed his faith in
Christ even as he was imprisoned and executed.*

3
YOU'LL DO ANYTHING

Charlie Brown is my favorite comic strip character. For those of you who didn't realize he was a comic strip figure, but only a TV star of sorts, you've gained some new trivia information. Linda gave me a little stuffed Charlie Brown dude for Christmas, and I love him. He's got a cute little face and a hairline just like mine. He sits in my study right next to me as my counselor, along with Abe Lincoln, Ulysses S. Grant, Robert E. Lee and George Washington. They're all hanging out in frames on the wall. Wow, what a brain trust. I also have a bust of the great reformer Martin Luther that sits on one of my bookcases. I just love hanging out and learning from all these guys. Believe it or not, some of the most profound lessons come from Charlie Brown. I guess you might say, "From one blockhead to another." My favorite Charlie Brown movie is *It's the Great Pumpkin, Charlie Brown*. The messages of love and commitment are right in your face. There are discussions within their small group about who exists, sacrificial love, and who's in charge. (It's Lucy, and we'll leave it at that).

But what about the sacrificial love and who really exists? Linus believes the Great Pumpkin really exists and he demonstrates his belief by his behavior. While everyone else is trick-or-treating, grabbing up the candy and having a blast at the party with the gang, he's in the pumpkin patch waiting for the Great Pumpkin. This guy believes! The dude is freezing his little bottom off and missing all the fun because he believes the Great Pumpkin is on the way. Okay, his motives might be a little messed up, but he sacrifices his reputation, fun, and candy for a creature that doesn't exist. This tiny figure of a man really has some faith.

The other lessons seem to come from Sally, who is hopelessly in love with Linus. She misses the whole deal too, because she's in love. It's goofy, and really doesn't make any sense, and that's exactly what appeals to me. Faith often doesn't make sense. "C'mon," you're saying, "this is a comic, a cartoon, a make believe story." Yep, but the lessons are still there in the lives of both Linus and Sally. In their own way, they demonstrate for everyone watching that belief dictates behavior. They're both willing to do anything for the object of their affections, and express their love with all their might! Even at the end of the movie when Charlie Brown asks Linus about his plans for the fall of next year, he's immoveable, uncompromising and not ashamed to proclaim his undying love and loyalty as he shouts, "I'll be in the pumpkin patch, waiting for the Great Pumpkin to rise up and bring toys to all the (believing) little girls and boys." That's almost word for word. His belief and commitment is obvious. You may think I'm off the wall, nuts, brain dead with this analogy, but I'm convinced it works. Think about it, you'll do anything for the one you love the most, and both Linus and Sally showed us that truth.

Jesus made that point very clear in Luke 14:25-33, and stories help us to think, even if they're just cartoons. Stories can help us process information and I enjoy telling them. It was a very effective part of Jesus' earthly ministry. Sometimes when I've been invited back to speak at a camp, church, or conference where I've been before, this situation may arise: "Hey, Chuck! I loved that story you told last year. I laughed so hard I fell off my chair. That story was awesome." I then look them right in their eyes and ask them, "So, what was the purpose of that story? What did it illustrate? Why did I tell it?" Often, their response is, "I don't know, but it was hysterical. I haven't laughed that hard in a long time." That's depressing for me to hear. It either

> *YOU'LL DO ANYTHING FOR THE ONE YOU LOVE THE MOST.*

means I'm a horrible communicator or they weren't listening to learn. Maybe it's because a whole year has gone by and it's just too much for them to remember. I love good stories and a good storyteller. I love to laugh, but sometimes humor gets in the way of getting the point of the story across to the audience. The story is designed to be a window for those who are listening. You want them to look into the window and grab some understanding.

Whenever I teach Luke 14:25-33 at some type of speaking engagement, I always finish with this story. No, not about the Great Pumpkin, but another one. It's a love story full of affection and romance. It is a story somewhat like Romeo and Juliet or Mickey and Minnie. Let the cameras roll and the story begin. But just so you won't forget why I'm telling it, and you're reading it, let me remind you. It's a window, an illustration and analogy of Luke 14:25-33. Continue on and you'll see what I mean.

In 1965, I was a freshman in high school—a babe of just thirteen—right in the middle of the turbulent years of the 1960's, perhaps the most destructive years in the history of our country. There were two distinct groups of students cruising the halls of any high school campus in the Chicagoland area. And the groups that walked the halls thought that they ruled the world. These groups had names that told you who they were and what their behavior was like. It's important to the story so we'll describe them one at a time.

The first group was called Dupers. Dupers wore Levi jeans, Madras shirts, sweat shirts and penny loafers. Penny Loafers were shoes and in '60s retro language, "They were BOSS!" The Duper community was comprised of lovers overall, not fighters. If you're hip to the evolution of that group, many became the "Long Hair Generation." From music to lumber jackets they were the non-aggressive types.

On the other hand, there were the Greasers, and they didn't like Dupers. They wore leather jackets, tee shirts, baggy blue or brown pants and pointy toed shoes, which could really hurt when used as a weapon. The two groups didn't get along. If you've ever watched old reruns of Happy Days, the Fonz is almost the perfect picture of a Greaser, except that he had a soft spot in his little Greaser heart. I want to make it clear before we go on in the story. The "Greaser" title had nothing to do with ethnicity and everything to do with their tough guy, bad boy image.

It was September of 1965 and I was walking the streets of Chicago on my way to high school. I already mentioned I was thirteen, a freshman, and also a proud Duper. I was wearing my red and black lumber jacket that was brand new, which made me a prime target for the Greaser boys. My mind was actively preoccupied with things that most guys of thirteen think about—girls and girls. I know you're all disappointed with me, but that's the real world for guys of that age. Oh yeah, football was in my head also; I loved it. For those of you wondering about the academic issue, it was in there somewhere, I think? My head was in the clouds as I strolled along singing Beach Boys songs. I was stoked, jacked up and excited. You know what all that means, right? As I turned the corner and took a look at the building where I'd spend the next four years of my life, I was overcome with fear. Not only did it look like a prison, but there seemed to be prison guards on the steps. Actually, at that moment prison guards would have been much better. It was a mob of leather jacketed Greasers looking for some food! Even though there were only about thirty or so of them, it was a traumatic first day of school moment. I thought to myself, "be calm and don't show them any signs of fear. Don't let them realize you're afraid." Those guys fed on that stuff and they could smell it.

Putting my head down trying to gain some composure, I thought I'd try another door. "I'll go in through another door and perhaps they'll never see me?" As I raised my head, I realized I was dead. They had already seen me and it was too late. My body reacted with an internal explosion of emotion, with heart pounding, cold sweat and shortness of breath. In those days, if you ran from the Greasers it would be worse for you. So all 120 pounds of me went forward to the sacrifice. Let me say this: nobody better call or email me with a loving rebuke about David and Goliath! I've already been there and heard that, but it would have been cool if I could have done that. It would have been a Duper first. But they were waiting for their food and must not be denied. Putting me in a circle I was hit, spit on, kicked and otherwise humiliated. It was just me against a whole bunch of bad boys and you'd better not cry. It was finally over and I was in an empty hallway on the first floor of the school. I'd been beaten up and now I was alone and lost. If anyone can understand bullying, I can.

Wandering around the school, I finally was directed to the third floor and my home room. The teacher's voice was stern and loud so I froze in the hallway. I told myself that I needed to just walk into the room and find a seat without making any commotion. I walked slowly through the doorway hoping not to been seen. What was I thinking, that I was still the little kid who would hide under his blanket and not be discovered? She, who would be my home room teacher for the next four years looked at me and said, "You're late, get out." I lunged out the door a basket case. Think about it, my first day as a freshman, beat up by Greasers, kicked out of class, on my way through puberty as a thirteen year old. Somebody help! I need counseling and a teddy bear or something to help me make it through life or at least this day.

She finally told me to come in the room and sit down. Full of anxiety, I slowly made my way toward my desk, when something incredible caught my eye. There in the front row of old wooden desks was my savior. With long dark hair and dark, dark eyes, she would make me forget about all the day's pain and become the savior of my life or a least that's how it felt. My energy was renewed and hope was growing in my mind. Was I a changed man? At thirteen, I embraced the challenge and set my course on a mission of love.

I pursued that girl with reckless abandon and creative methods. If you could hum the *Mission Impossible* song in your head at this moment, it would create a great soundtrack for the story as you read on. My mission of love in focus now, I found her schedule and began stalking her. It was legal back then... I think? Waiting for her, I'd pop out from around a corner and quickly ask if I could carry her books or something. Sometimes I would mumble my words, but I didn't care. You see, *you'll do anything for the one you love the most*. Say that out loud three times, and then read on.

My plans were carefully thought out; I wanted this girl. I was very stealthy, covert, prepared to gain the victory. Her lunch period was the same time as mine. I'd sneak up behind her, get on my knees, grab her hand and sing a love song with passion. The enemy—her girlfriends—would begin to whack at me ferociously with their hands or anything they could find. They were using artillery and their shells were exploding in my face. I fought off the blows to my head and continued to sing to her with all my might. "When I woke up this morning you were on my mind, you were on my mind, my mind." I was dodging the blows, but wouldn't stop. Believe it or not I think there were times I even quoted Shakespeare, some *Romeo and Juliet*. Poised and confident I'd begin with, "She doth teach the torches to burn bright, seems as though she hangs upon a cheek of night as a rich jewel in an Ethiop's ear beauty too rich for use for earth too dear. So shows a snowy dam trooping with crows as yonder lady or her fellow shows. Did my heart love till now? For swear it sight. I ne'er saw true beauty till this night." Girls love it... well, maybe?

Sometimes when I'm out speaking and I break into these lines the reaction is wild. I don't think it's my performance as much as it is the crowd thinking, "Man you were crazy to do that. Did you actually do that?" I know you're reading this, and it's not a live event, but say it in your head again or out loud: *you'll do anything for the one you love the most!*

I stalked, sang, quoted, her girlfriends beat me, but I wouldn't stop pursuing the object of my love. And after two whole years of hard work and labor (did you get that? Two years!), I asked her on a date, and she said, "YES!" I went out of my mind. Now before you draw any conclusions here, let me clarify. I'm not promoting dating. Perhaps that's yet another book!

So back to being out of my mind and the date—our first date. We went to an amusement park in Chicago and now she was holding my hand. I think I was drooling and trying not to act too silly but, the one I loved the most was holding my hand. The night was spent riding rides, eating hot dogs and engaging in teenage conversation. At one point, she asked me if I'd ride any ride she liked. Without hesitation, I blurted yes, anything of course, whatever you want to ride. She pointed towards a group of rides and said. "That one, right there." My response was immediate, "Let's go get in line." I grabbed her hand and off we went. As we were running toward the ride I shouted that I love roller coasters. The Bobs was my favorite. It was the fastest at the park and had the steepest hills. She suddenly stopped which caused us to almost tumble to the ground. I said, "What are you doing?" Her beautiful dark eyes looked up at me and she said, "No, no, not the Bobs, but the one behind it." I slowly lifted my eyes and saw a tower reaching almost 300 feet straight up into the night sky. The ride was called the Parachutes and it terrified me. You sat on a piece of something with a little strap I think over your lap and up you went, almost 300 feet in the air. I promise you rides were built a whole lot different back then. It wasn't quite the Dark Ages, but it was close. Trust me, it was scary, and I thought I would die. If you ever get to hear me tell this story in person, I'll give you more horrifying details. She continued to say, "I love it. It tickles my stomach." In silence I was thinking, "It might be tickling your stomach, but mine's ready to toss!"

It's incredible, isn't it? We'll do anything—can you finish it by now? She was the person that controlled me. I'd suffer any *persecution* for her and spend everything that was in my possession, for a human being who had no power to give real life, eternal life. Think about that statement for a moment. Up, up, up and up we went, dangling on a wing and a prayer. I forgot to mention this: when the ride hits the top, it free falls. It begins to descend rapidly, constantly picking up speed, faster and faster until it reaches the ground. There was a parachute that *should* open at some point and slow the ride down, but you never knew when that would happen. That's what she loved about the ride, the surprise. All I thought about were three things: Number one, I'd throw up on her. Number two, my bladder would explode all over her. Number three, it would be a simultaneous reaction, and with that the date would be over. I pictured her telling her parents, "Look what he did to me. I'm a mess!" All would be lost!

The fear I experienced on that ride was almost life-shattering, but...*you'll do anything for the one you love the most*. Wow, I can't believe I did that. But I wanted to prove my love for that girl. We had both survived without catastrophe and we dated for two more years. Fast forward to our senior year and I thought we were still in love or something like it. We even had a song off the radio—*Never My Love*—and it was our song. We wore each other's high school rings and seemed to always be together. Surprisingly, one day in front of my house in beautiful Chicago, we had a lovers' spat. We'd had a few before, so I didn't think much of it at the moment. She took my ring off her finger and tossed it at me and said, "I don't love you anymore." I said, "You don't mean that!" Her response was, "I do mean it" and she turned to walk away. You talk about being devastated, or in 1960s lingo, blown away. I was rocked. I shot back in complete panic, "If you leave, I'll..." Before I could finish what I was about to say, she shot back, "You'll do what? What?" Remember our little phrase? You'll do anything for the one you love the most. I said, "I'll kill myself!" Teenage love, what an emotional mess. She turned, stuck out her hip the way females do when they're serious and shouted, "Go ahead." When females do that hip thing, it's scary. Even when my mom did it, I knew I was in big trouble. I think it's their exclamation point or something like that. The one I would do anything for called my bluff. It was a real bummer.

I needed to say or do something right away. So I yelled back, "Alright, watch this." There was a car coming down our narrow street. I know, you're saying, "Chuck you idiot, you're not really going to do this, are you?" Remember, when love is real, it's a blood for blood deal, and at least I could make it look good. Watching the car carefully I was convinced I could time it perfectly and make it look like the car really hit me. She would see my dramatic expression of love (or stupidity) and reconsider. The car was getting closer and I knew my timing was crucial to staying alive. What was I thinking? You know how some comedians say to be successful as a comedian your timing is key? It must be spot on! Well, mine was a hair off and the car nailed me. OOPS! Before I knew it I was doing a 360° in the air. My life and thoughts flashed all over the place as I said to myself, "I really don't want to die." It was too late and I freaked as I landed on the hood of the car. I did a face plant on the windshield, mouth wide open. The kid driving the car slammed on the brakes. What would you do at a moment like that? It wasn't like a little birdie went plop on the window. It was a big bird—me!

With the sudden stop of the car, I went airborne again. Finally landing on the Chicago pavement, I was almost knocked out. When I gathered myself and realized I was still in the land of the living, it felt a little better. Then I began to look at my body to see what might be missing! I thought for a minute that I might end up like the Scarecrow in *The Wizard of Oz*, shouting, "My legs are over there and my arms are over there." I was a mess. I also thought rats would begin to pour out of the sewers, licking up my yummy blood! The next thing I saw was the car's driver standing over me screaming wildly, "Are you all right? Are you all right?" He seemed to be in worse shape than I was at the moment. I was fine and I told him to get away from me, go away and leave me alone. You see I knew she was coming, the one I loved the most was coming. So I screamed, "Get away!" She must have heard or seen my incredible expression of love. She'll be here. I didn't move. I just laid there and laid there and laid there and laid there.

She never came. It seemed like an eternity. All my sacrifice, all my love. Stalking, singing, Shakespeare, life-threatening rides. You'll do *anything*...for the one you love the most. Blood for blood, but she never came back, at least not on that particular day. But she did eventually, and she's still my girl to this day. Did you get it? It's Linda, my wife. She's been the love of my life since I was thirteen. She was the girl I stalked, sang to and almost died for. She's "MY GIRL" as the Temptations sang. I've been talking about my girl. I've been blessed and grateful to our LORD for our story and relationship. Our song is still *Never My Love* and when we're home and not out speaking we listen to it every Saturday morning. I love her and am committed until death do us part.

But, I didn't tell you the story to make you think about us and our relationship. I told you the story so you can evaluate your love for Christ. Often when I am out speaking, people get confused about this. They don't understand the point of this story about Linda and me. They want to think more about Linda and me than their relationship with Christ. Once again, the story is designed to illustrate the fact that we will do anything for the one we love the most, and that must be Jesus. In reality, there's no human being that can do what Jesus has done to save us. So, it makes sense, doesn't it? He alone deserves our supreme love and devotion.

The story is about Him! It's about Luke 14:25-33. The stories that you just read were used as practical examples of the powerful words Jesus taught those following Him. He told them from His heart to theirs that you'll do anything for the one you love the most. It was non-negotiable, no options, no alternatives. He must be the ONE and the ONLY ONE they submit their lives to. For all of us today, embracing His demands proves our faith in Jesus and demonstrates that our love for Him is real. It's the supernatural mark of God on and in our lives! It is that Divine imprint which declares to a watching world, "I'm His and He's the ONE I love the most!"

JESUS PAID IT ALL, ALL TO HIM I OWE.
E.M. HALL

4
THAT VALUABLE STUFF CALLED TIME

Tick tock, tick tock. Who owns your clock? In chapter one, I briefly mentioned the word *apps*. I said we'd find our way to them eventually. I think we're all familiar with the term, at least in one way or another. I'd like to use it a little bit differently than perhaps all of us are used to. The next few chapters will focus on giving practical applications to Jesus' teaching in Luke 14:25-33. The apps will begin to put flesh on doctrine that can be difficult to grasp intellectually, emotionally and spiritually. Let's go to app #1: that valuable stuff called time!

You've heard this statement before, "You'll do anything for the One you love the most." It's my summary of what Jesus was teaching the crowds in Luke 14:25-33. You may disagree with me, but I think I'm right. The one you love the most gets your time. You've heard the old cliché that time is money. When I was in sales before entering ministry, I had that quoted at me regularly. I've also heard, "Whatever gets the majority of your time is what's really valuable to you." So, what's really valuable to you? Who, or what, gets your time?

When Linda and I were dating in high school and college, who do you think captured my time? I don't have to answer. You've already answered it by now. It was absolutely incredible! Both of us would do almost anything to be together—I mean crazy stuff. Love finds a way, you know! We lived approximately two miles apart in the heart of Chicago. We wanted to see each other one day, but it seemed there was no way to

THE ONE YOU LOVE THE MOST GETS YOUR TIME.

make it happen. Neither one of us had a car at our disposal, so we were stuck. The temperature that night was below zero, but if I could make it happen we'd steal a few precious minutes together. I decided to make it work, and in a flash I was out the door running down Cicero Avenue toward her house. My pace increased as I realized our time would be short because my parents didn't want me out that night. We'll talk about the obedience topic later in another chapter. The point is, I had very little time to spend with the one I loved the most, and that time was priceless.

Finally reaching her house, I tried to move my fingers, but they seemed to be frozen. The door opened and there she was staring at me in amazement. We hurried inside and sat down at her kitchen table, her eyes still expressing shock. Then she asked, "How did you get here?" I tried to respond, but my face was still frozen at that point. I made a creaking noise that sounded like the Tin Man in *The Wizard of Oz*. She asked me again saying, "Why did you do this? What's wrong with you?" My face was now thawing and beginning to really hurt. I tried to tell her the best I could what I was trying to say, but it wasn't working. I was squeaking and mumbling and leaking, not making sense at all. Little by little the words came together. I kept saying over and over in my arctic language, "I ran... because I love you."

Her face began to smile, and her eyes glistened as she understood what I was saying. She understood that for me to get a few minutes of time with her, I'd do anything. Hypothermia was no obstacle. I'd do anything for just a second with her, to look into her eyes. Those valuable minutes together interfacing and sharing "sweet nothings" were worth any sacrifice. The relationship we had was the most precious, valuable thing in my life. I'd do almost anything to be with her! As valuable as my time was, I wanted her to get it all if possible.

Jesus was clearly telling the crowd, "If you really love me, I'll get your time. You'll begin to reorganize your life and I'll become the priority of it." Let's face it. Our lives are so busy and cluttered we can barely find time to take a deep breath. If you're a teenager there's school, homework, sports, friends, jobs, parental demands, siblings to watch, parties, texts to send and receive, cars to care for, movies to watch. Man, life is nuts! If you're a parent, life is even more hectic. And if you are a young parent with babies, the diapers never end. In a very real sense, your responsibilities are overwhelming.

For the rest of you, it's not a whole lot better. To find time for anything else amidst our busy, wild, almost frantic schedules seems practically impossible. Did I forget to mention church, youth group, community groups, life groups, small groups, worship teams, children's ministries, deacon meetings, elder meetings, committee meetings and so on? I have no doubt I've missed something that eats up your time. Life is full, isn't it? By the way, did you fix the broken toilet?

I think the point I'm trying to make has been successfully communicated. Whether it's school, occupation, social activities, church functions or relationships, we need to spend time with Jesus first. But our intimate time with Jesus is tough to find. Our time seems to be gone with the wind. It's devoured and digested by the tyrannical monsters of daily life.

All of the activities I listed earlier are not necessarily wrong or bad. To have friends is good, and taking time to express your love for them is great. Making changes in your schedule to show them you really care and are concerned about their lives seems normal. Giving them first place and priority over your plans for the day is an appropriate sacrifice. To spend time listening to them and unselfishly doing whatever it takes to meet their needs is an expression of your love. Protecting and providing for them in a right and pure way demonstrates your brotherly love for them. It is one of the greatest joys in this life to have a friend or friends like I just described.

Human friendship, true friendship, is rare and should be treasured and protected. Educational experiences, occupational opportunities that provide for us the resources to live, along with recreational activities are healthy for us and should be viewed as gifts. Social media used wisely is fun and entertaining. Church activities have the ability to really enhance and encourage our lives for our good. The point I'm trying to make is this: when any of these good relationships or activities replace our time with Christ, they subtly take priority and become the one we love the most.

Some of you might be thinking or asking the question, "Are you saying my church activities are not an expression of my love for Christ?" I'm going to be lovingly careful here, but not afraid to say what I think. I can't really say, because I don't have the power to look into your mind. First of all, I don't know everyone who will read this book. Second, I remember what Jesus told the religious leaders of His day. He tossed at them a bunch of audible "woes" against their

THE DANGER IS DECEIVING OURSELVES INTO BELIEVING THAT OUR BUSY ACTIVITY IS ALWAYS REAL LOVE FOR JESUS.

religious activity. Religious activity does not necessarily prove our love for Him. On the other hand, it may. The danger is deceiving ourselves into believing that our busy activity is always real love for Jesus.

Remember the story of Mary and Martha in Luke 10? Read the text carefully.

Luke 10:38-42 English Standard Version (ESV)

38 Now as they went on their way, Jesus entered a village. And a woman named Martha welcomed him into her house. 39 And she had a sister called Mary, who sat at the Lord's feet and listened to his teaching. 40 But Martha was distracted with much serving. And she went up to him and said, "Lord, do you not care that my sister has left me to serve alone? Tell her then to help me." 41 But the Lord answered her, "Martha, Martha, you are anxious and troubled about many things, 42 but one thing is necessary. Mary has chosen the good portion, which will not be taken away from her."

I don't want to write out a sermon here and you probably don't want me to preach at you. So, I'm asking you to think with me. One of my mentors from years gone by taught me to ask questions and make observations of the text you're studying to gain insight. So here are some brief observations and questions. The story speaks of Jesus and two sisters. One was worried and anxious and the other sat listening at Jesus' feet. I hope they were clean! Martha makes a demand of Jesus. Mary continues to sit. Jesus rebukes Martha. Jesus commends Mary. Mary seems to have received something that will never be taken away.

I have another question to ask and think about. Which sister loved Jesus? Maybe it should be asked this way, "Which one loved Him the most?" I don't think that's the lesson here. Maybe we're supposed to think about it this way. Martha was a good, faithful hostess but she missed it. Remember, Jesus rebuked her so we really can't justify her actions. Preachers have trashed the text, me included at times. I think it's because so many of us are "Marthas" and we believe busy, busy, busy is good. But Jesus told Mary she got it right. She had reorganized her day for Him. He got her time! She probably had things to do, just like Martha. Instead she chose to put them aside and sit at the feet of Jesus and listen to God in the flesh. The One she loved the most was there and she wouldn't miss the moment. She had learned that intimate worship of her Lord must be the priority of her life.

Somehow we need to figure out a way to do what Mary did every day. You might be saying, "Well, if Jesus showed up physically at my house, I'd sit at His feet too." You wouldn't sit, you'd pass out! Jesus made it clear in Luke 14. He was telling the crowd what you love most, gets most of your time. It's there; think about it.

David the giant-killer is my favorite Bible character, besides Jesus. He wasn't a perfect king, husband, father, friend or brother. He messed up big! Maybe that's why I dig him so much. All you need to do is read the Psalms and you'll discover who he loved the most and who got the majority of his time. It seems as though his mind was consumed with God. I love the Psalms! People ask me often, "What's your favorite?" "All of them," I shout back, "all of them." I do have a couple of special ones and maybe they're your favorites also. I love Psalm 62 and 63. They both beautifully express the love David had for his God. Charles Spurgeon calls Psalm 62, "the only Psalm." Over and over David cries from his heart words that tell all the world, God alone was the one he loved the most. In Psalm 63, he gives us the pattern of his daily disciplines. It begins with, "O God, you are my God; earnestly I seek you."

Without sermonizing here, he makes it clear God got his time, from early morning until the day was done and the lamps had burned out. My opinion is that David dreamt about God and His Truth. His mind was consumed with the one he loved the most. He was a busy man, king, father, husband, but he had learned to make time for intimate moments with his God. He had learned the Biblical art of meditation and private worship. He loved the Shepherd of his soul and nothing would take the place of time with Him. Maybe if we could be shepherds on the little hills of Bethlehem for a few years, we'd learn what's really important in this life? I often thought how cool it would be to hang out where David did for months.

Please understand something about me. I have not mastered app #1 in my life, but I want to. I want to know my God and grow in my relationship with Him. The Psalmist says in Psalm 16:11, "in Your presence there is fullness of joy." Besides the truth that giving your time in a Biblical pattern to Jesus proves your love is real, the benefits are of earthly and eternal value. Think hard about app #1. It's absolutely essential if we claim to be disciples of Jesus. We choose where we will spend our time.

Before I crawl into your space, I'll confess a bit. I love football, March Madness, reading, yard work and I could go on. I'll give hours, I mean hours on any given day to these. None of them are by nature evil. But any of these can become an idol in my life and that is evil. How you ask? The answer is easy, but tough to evaluate with our hearts that are often very deceiving. When I give more time to any of these than my time with Jesus, I've got a problem. Think! If you could watch my life or hear my thoughts without me knowing you'd be able to evaluate who gets my time. Your reaction to this is probably something like this, "That's wrong," and you're right. We don't need to create any more legalistic church mafia. But if you could do it, you'd find out where my time goes. Scary isn't it? And let's face it, none of us want to be involved in a church spy ring. All of us would be exposed to whom and what we love the most. What's getting mucho, lots, too much of our time would be revealed. Electronic toys such as phones (the smart ones of course) and tablets and computers that can cause insanity of sorts eat away precious moments in all of our relationships. Then there's television, movies, sports, exercise. The idols of time could go on. For some it's relationships of all types. Some parents have made their children time-idols. Some have made occupation and education time-idols.

Jesus never told the crowd, "Don't enjoy life and the relationships that are in it." He wants us to find pleasure in the majesty of His creation, and that takes time. He has given us wonderful earthly companions to enjoy life with, and that takes time. He's given us minds that can grow and technology that can be used for His glory, and that takes time. I can't fix your time issues—that's your problem. But the fact still remains, whomever or whatever you love the most gets your time. Remember the story of Mary. He wants us to be like her.

IF I COULD SAVE TIME IN A BOTTLE
THE FIRST THING THAT I'D LIKE TO DO
IS TO SAVE EVERY DAY TILL ETERNITY PASSES AWAY
JUST TO SPEND THEM WITH YOU
JIM CROCE

POINTS to PONDER

1. Do you believe the text is really teaching that the one you love the most gets the priority of your time? Was this really Christ's challenge?
2. Is it realistic and humanly possible to meet His TIME demand?
3. A true disciple of Jesus is always evaluating his or her time distribution.
4. Many of us squeeze out time for Jesus when it's convenient. Agree or disagree? Explain your answer to yourself out loud.
5. Can you identify something that has become the one you love the most and needs to go? And why?
6. When unbelievers see believers who are not controlled and consumed with the same passions they have, what response might it cause?
7. Who do you relate to the most in your daily patterns of life: Mary or Martha? Explain your answer to yourself out loud.

5
IF YOU LOVE ME, TALK TO ME

Who do you talk to the most? I need to explain myself for a minute before I deal with that question. Some of you reading this book might mistakenly come to the conclusion that this book is all about Linda and Chuck, and not about following Jesus. I've thought about that a lot, and I need to make sure we're all on the same page. Occasionally somebody will say, "You must have really loved Linda to get hit by a car and all the other crazy stuff you did for her." I respond with, "I still love her and do all kinds of crazy things for her but, I don't do cars anymore!"

You see I'm convinced that human relationships in the proper context are great illustrations of our relationship with the Godhead. We'll go to some wild extremes for those we love. With that being explained, and hopefully understood, our story goes on to illustrate that you'll do anything for the one you love the most. So, back to the question that began this chapter. Who do you talk to the most? It should be the one you love the most.

When I was in high school, we lived in a cool old house. It had all kinds of freaky places to hide and pop out to just about give someone a heart attack. I loved that house. We also had big black water bugs that lived somewhere in the dark places of that home. Many times I'd come home late at night and all of the lights would be off. It was pitch black. It was my time with my little black water bug friends. If you quietly sneaked in and turned the kitchen light on, they'd be all over the kitchen floor. The race was on! I would see how many I could mush before they disappeared back to their secret dwellings, hopefully not in my bedroom. It was awesome, just like playing a video game on the floor. After I'd finished with my mushing, I would leave the bodies of the dead victims to show my mother what a good and faithful son I was— the protector of our homeland.

Sorry, I got distracted for a moment, but wasn't it fun? There is a point to that story and here it is: Besides spending time on that floor chasing creepy creatures, I spent time chasing a beautiful girl. I know you're wondering how that all worked. There was a door right off the kitchen that went to the basement and the flooring was all the same. Many nights I would sit on that same floor right inside the door in deep conversation, and of course, in the dark. I could have been covered by my little friends or perhaps even eaten alive by them. But there was nothing that would prevent me from holding my ground, it was my space. The old ancient phone cord stretched just enough so I could talk and hold the door shut tight. You see I was speaking to the one I loved the most and nobody would interrupt that important time. Many tried, but there was no way! With all my strength I'd hold the door handle while my Dad would try to pry the door open. But, it wasn't going to happen. You're wondering if I was being a bad and rebellious son, aren't you? I don't think I was. But I know this for sure—you'll do anything for the one you love the most—even battle your father for the phone.

If you're thinking I'm becoming too repetitious with that statement, I've only just begun. It's at the core of our lives—who we love the most. So we talked on the phone, and we talked on the phone, and we talked as long as possible. There were times that five hours would be considered a short conversation. My parents would ask

HE DOESN'T WANT TO BE CRAMMED INTO YOUR DAY FOR A QUICK "TEXT MESSAGE". HE WANTS TO BE THE PRIORITY OF RELATIONAL INTERACTION IN YOUR LIFE.

me, and I'm sure Linda's asked her, "What do you guys have to talk about for all that time?" Really? Did they forget so soon? I know for a fact that anyone in love, especially at the beginning of their relationship, can talk for a long, long, time! So what did Linda and I talk about all of that time on the phone? I'm not going to tell you and neither will she, except in big generalities. It's quite amazing, there were actually times we were silent. Those personal moments, reflective and quiet, were simply another expression of our affection for each other. She was on the other end of the line and I was on mine, and the relationship was alive.

We did speak tons of words that would encourage each other, and we asked questions about each other's day. Of course, being a little bit of the jealous type, I wanted to make certain nobody else was getting her conversation, especially a guy. So I investigated that a bit, and in her own way so did she. We made plans for the next day and discussed our future dreams. Looking back on those conversations, we really were involved in each other's lives. Teenage sweethearts now married for many years and a relationship still developing. We can still talk for hours about a whole bunch of topics ranging from family to history to sports and our love for one another. But it always comes back to what holds us together and gives us hope—our relationship with Jesus.

We love talking about Him and of course communicating with Him. Prayer is at the center of our lives and that's really what's at the core of this chapter. In our human relationships, we love to talk to those we love and express our commitment to them. If Jesus is the One we love the most, it makes sense that He would be the One we converse with the most. It may sound a little silly to you, but in today's terms, He should get our phone and text time.

If you're feeling guilty, welcome to the club. The priority of this book was not to make you feel good, but to challenge you to evaluate your commitment to Christ in direct response to Luke 14:25-33. If you're thinking hard about His words in that text, He was making it clear. "Don't say you love me, if you won't spend your time in intimate conversation with Me." This is app #2. He desires and demands us to lovingly talk and interact with Him. He doesn't want to be crammed into your day for a quick "text message." He wants to be the priority of relational interaction in your life.

The disciples saw the intimate, loving conversation between Jesus and His Father, and they said, "Teach us to pray." I really don't want to beat up on you about your weak prayer life—I don't know all of you. Some of you perhaps could do a great job with this chapter, better than me. But that's not the point. The powerful challenge from Jesus is, in my own words, "TALK TO ME!" Let's face reality about this delicate issue in our lives. All of us avoid those that we don't want to interact with or be with. But it's a fact that we'll all go out of our way, and reorganize our lives, to speak to someone with whom we have a valuable relationship.

While I've been writing this book at different locations, I can't help but watch people. I'm somewhat of a coffee snob, so you know some of my writing haunts. It's amazed me! I'll be in a coffee shop for hours working, and of course getting caffeinated up. Some people are there for the same amount of time, talking. For hours and hours, they interact—face to face and ear to ear. The conversation goes on and on and on. I probably shouldn't work in that environment—I have big ears.

It's hard sometimes not to get caught up in their talkie talk. The stuff you hear is frightening, hysterical and flat-out dumb. I can't believe people have so much time to talk about crazy stuff. I do, however, occasionally grab a good illustration or two. I'm not saying that we shouldn't have human conversations, especially with those we love. What I am asking you to do is this: examine who gets the most valuable conversation in your life. You will talk most to the person in your life you value the most.

Years ago when I was being booked to speak,

sometimes three years in advance, it seemed a bunch of people wanted to talk to me. I think they thought I was relatively important or something. My conversation and time with them appeared to be valuable and very important. We would talk for hours upon hours. When my popularity in the speaking and training world seemed to decrease, the relationships with many, but not everyone, changed. Time in conversation with certain individuals was seemingly no longer desired. Perhaps what they were looking for was gone. What they thought would be advantageous to them disappeared. I no longer had much to offer in the way of benefiting them.

If this sounds like I'm having a pity party, I'm not. I think all of us are guilty of this sad commentary on humanity. So in the same way, the One who we say is our Lord knows the motives of our hearts and conversation with Him. I thank Him for His compassion and patience in my life. Too often, my conversation with Him has been me-centered. I have talked, conversed or prayed only when it was advantageous to me.

Our God wants words of love and adoration from His children. Sometimes I'll read the cute notes our sons would give me when they were just little boys. I laugh with joy at their expressions of love for me. I really love reading them, as they bring tremendous encouragement to my day. When they take some time out of their busy lives and call to talk, I love it. I know they've reorganized their day to interact with me and that's big! You've got to figure this out for yourselves and how to make it work daily for you. App #2 is absolutely vital to our spiritual development. It's also proof of who it is we love the most when it's directed by God's Word.

Prayer is more than just a phrase in a bulletin, a

worship celebration, the blessing of a meal or a routine exercise of a religious demand. Prayer with the One we love the most is the affectionate daily, hourly, ongoing interaction between us and our God that's driven by our love for Him. So, find your place, fill your mind, express your love and build that relationship with the One you love the most. And remember, you don't need a dark kitchen and an army of little black water bugs to make this happen.

PRAYER WITH THE ONE WE LOVE THE MOST IS THE AFFECTIONATE DAILY, HOURLY, ONGOING INTERACTION BETWEEN US AND OUR GOD THAT'S DRIVEN BY OUR LOVE FOR HIM.

POINTS to PONDER

1. Prayer conversation is the mark of a true disciple of Christ!
2. Who do you talk to the most in your daily life, and why?
3. We are religious people with little relational passion for our God. Agree or disagree? Explain your answer to yourself.
4. It's my responsibility to figure this out if Jesus is the ONE I love the most.

P.S. Linda loves to get a blank card with my personalized, special words of love instead of a store-bought commercial message card. Think about it.

6
WHAT'S IN THE BOX?

We have an eleven year-old grandson. He's a bud, a dude. He rocks. His name is Travis, and like all eleven year-olds, he loves to get presents. We love to wrap them up in all types of boxes and packages and give them to him. Sometimes we get goofy with the gifts and he looks at us like we're nuts. Well, there is a little bit of crazy in both of us—grandma and grandpa. He calls me "Papa" and I love it. We love to have fun and be wacko at times, especially when we're together with him. What's wacko? Google it.

I remember a couple of years ago we gave him a drum set for his birthday. He's got rhythm just like me, I think? It was a big deal so we waited to give him the drums as the last gift of the party. I carefully snuck out of the party to get the drums out of our car. I began to haul the wrapped drums into the house as quietly as possible without being seen by him. His eyes were wide with anticipation and excitement as I placed the packages before his jumping little body. He could hardly control himself as he wondered, "What's in the box?"

Finally, he was given the green light and the ripping started. Paper was flying all over the place as he was frantically at work. We've all been in his shoes and it's a heart-pounding, thrilling moment as we wonder, "What's in the box?" He exploded with shouts of satisfaction and joy, "Drums, drums, drums! I've got a drum set." He wanted those drums to be set up as soon as possible so he could beat those babies. Of course, that's daddy's job, so we all stepped aside and waited. Travis lunged at us and gave us a loving stranglehold of thanks. It was much better than the other stranglehold I told you about earlier. Then, the beating started—his first drum solo. And it's gotten better and better since then. He was enjoying the gift he had asked for, and we loved watching him play. He'd wanted those drums for a long time and now he was pounding them with a look of great satisfaction. Wow!

As grandparents, it was a blast watching him pound and play his heart out with his new, loud gift. We always try to find out what he really wants and surprise him with that special gift. He's not a spoiled little punk. He's always grateful for whatever we give him. And whatever we give him, he knows it's been wrapped with all of our love.

All of us love to give gifts to people that we love; it's just the natural thing to do. We love giving special gifts to special people in our lives. We'll save, sacrifice, and search out to find the perfect gift for them. The ones we love so very much should get gifts that have been specially selected and wrapped for them—tangible expressions that say, "You're the one. I love you very, very much!"

I think about this all the time. Who should get the best gifts from me? Some of you are thinking, "That's not hard to figure out. The answer is me, myself and I!" Let's face it. We all can understand the desire to accumulate more and more stuff for ourselves. We love our possessions, and we love ourselves, which makes it difficult to give our best to those around us.

My dad had a little drawer in his bedroom that was always loaded with candy. But for some reason, I never really got to enjoy those treats. Sometimes I'd go sneaking around to find that little drawer of treasures, but in the process of hunting, I would never find the place where "X" marked the spot. I think my dad moved his little drawer from place to place because he wanted it for himself and didn't want to share it with his kids. You might be thinking, "What a horrible father!" I knew he loved us and at times he would give us a little piece. But we never got full access to that delectable storehouse of sugary treats.

My dad, like all of us, struggled with selfishness and possessions (the "me, myself and I" in all of us). He wanted to give, but he didn't want to sacrifice what he considered the best of his stuff—things—the objects of his pleasure and affections. Like all of us, he sometimes struggled and held back his best instead of giving it to those he said he loved so very much. What's incredible to me is the realization that I've developed a little drawer of my own—a storehouse for myself. How sick is that? All of us really struggle with selfishness, don't we? Do you have a "me only" drawer?

In Luke 14, knowing the heart of mankind, Jesus addressed the issue of possessions and selfishness. He accurately shoots another arrow to our hearts which can be consumed with self-indulgent and self-gifting attitudes. (We all like selfies!) His arrow hits the center and splits our emotions wide open as He states, "I want your best gifts." He wants all of us to contemplate and consider this powerful demand. He's not saying we can give gifts only to Him, and never to anyone else. That kind of thinking would contradict His teaching. What He is saying is this: "I want and deserve the best, even that which is stored away in your 'little drawer.' I want you, as My child, to sacrifice, to seek out and serve Me with your best gifts of love."

In the New Testament, Ephesians 5:8-10 says this, "for at one time you were darkness, but now you are light in the Lord. Walk as children of light for the fruit of light is found in all that is good and right and true, and try to discern what is pleasing to the Lord."

Let's make some brief observations and ask some questions about the text. Paul tells the people he's writing, "at one time you were darkness." These same people are "light in the Lord." So, the people who were dark are now light. I don't think it has anything to do with the physical attributes of these people, do you?

Let's ask this question, "Dark is bad and light is good, right?" It sounds like these people were changed internally and now they have new desires in life. Oops, have I slipped into interpretation? Do you think Paul is reminding them of what they were and who they are now? He talks about walking differently than before—a life that is good, right and true. Then he says something like this: I want you to find out what pleases God. Do you think he's stating that God has a desire to receive special gifts from His children, wrapped up the way He likes them? Take some time and chew on this. If God is relational and desires a relationship with His people, wouldn't He want gifts of love from His own family members?

Listen carefully! I never said He needed, but wanted. He wants gifts of love from those whom He's saved as expressions of gratitude and praise for His work in them. He wants us to work hard at discerning, digging, and finding out what pleases Him. I remember wanting to give Linda a special gift when we were dating. First of all, I wanted to give her something that told the world, especially all the other guys, "Back off, she's mine." I had no money, but I would do whatever it took to make it happen. So, I sold the stamp collection I had been working on for years. If my parents would have ever found out, it would have been a life sentence of teenage grounding. Boy! Imagine if I had that book of stamps now?!

I took the money, bought her a wrist bracelet and had our names engraved on it. I showed the world she was mine. Through a process of asking her questions, I found out things she loved. Of course, she was the one I loved the most and I wanted to please her. She loved yellow long stem roses and chocolate. Nothing has changed about those two items over the years together. She still loves to get both of them as gifts and seems to never get bored with my efforts. I think part of the reason why is that she knows they're from me. In her mind, she knows this: I've been thinking about her and I've taken time out of my day to make the effort to please her. Through the years I've come to this conclusion about the chocolate—the darker, the better. Some of you might say dark—that's gross. For my girl it's dark, dark and darker and that's all that matters. You see, I've taken the time to find that out about her.

The same principle applies to Jesus and His disciples. Reflecting again on Paul's words to the Ephesians, he states clearly, "Find out what is pleasing to God." In my own words, "We are to figure out what gift from us pleases God the most." Doesn't it make sense? If Jesus is the One we love the most, what gift does He want the most from us?

Listen to His own words from the Gospel of John. He gives us a big clue beginning in 14:15. He says, "If you love Me, you will keep My commandments." Jesus then tells His guys about the Holy Spirit and His relationship to them. But again, in verse 21 He says, "Whoever has my commandments and KEEPS them, he it is who loves Me." Once again, He speaks of His and the Father's

THE PERFECT GIFT FOR OUR GOD IS OBEDIENCE, MOTIVATED BY LOVE.

relationship with those who will love and obey. He then says in verse 23, "If anyone loves Me, he will keep My word." He finishes the verse with this incredible promise to those who do what He asks of them. He says, "and My Father will love him and we will come to him and make our home with him."

I'm telling you this with my feeble, finite, little mind which is always theologically challenged. The perfect gift for our God is obedience, motivated by love. That's what He wants from us more than anything else. He wants us to wrap up our obedience in our own unique way and live it out in our daily lives. He doesn't want us to be copycats who try to duplicate what others give Him. He wants it to be from our heart to His. Listen to what He says in 14:24, "Whoever does not love Me, does not keep My words." OUCH! It screams so clearly in my mind, "obedience, obedience, obedience. That's the gift He wants." Wrap it up practically any way you'd like every day and minute of your life. The perfect gift in the box is one that's driven by love and thoughtfully and intentionally delivered as an act of loving obedience. It's *all* love and nothing else.

It almost sounds like too much loving, right? But if you think hard about it for a moment, how could that ever be? Over and over again, Jesus told that to the people following Him in many different teaching situations. I don't want your heartless, lack of love, and sacrificial religious rituals which can never save you. I want you to live your lives in loving obedience, proving to the world you've been saved by Me. And the response to My loving work in your life is your gift of adoration, thanks and praise by lovingly obeying My words. This is app #3. I'm convinced He wants us to demonstrate a heart of sacrificial gift-giving.

Years ago we wanted to take a family vacation, but we didn't have the finances to make it happen at the time. So we decided to have a garage sale and raise some dollars to go. We've all most likely visited a garage sale or two—lots of junk for sale. It's normally stuff we all want to get rid of and make some money off of in the process. You've heard the saying that one man's junk is another man's treasure. As we were putting out our junk on the tables for display, I noticed our youngest son bringing out some *Star Wars* items. He set up a little display that was incredible. We talked about it for a while and came to a decision about selling his precious stuff. Even though it was a painful sacrifice for him, he wanted to do it for the family. He put out some of his most valuable figures to sell in order to raise funds for our family trip. It was really a big sacrifice and I can still see him saying goodbye to some of those little figures and villages. Goodbye, Yoda. So long, Han. See ya, little Ewoks. I'll miss ya, Chewie.

It was amazing for a dad to watch his son set an example for all of us in loving, sacrificial giving. He gave all our family a wonderful gift. We went on vacation together and had a blast. What a gift! I'll never forget that as his father. All these years later, this story still brings tears to my eyes. I'm not saying it wasn't difficult for him to sell his valuable possessions. Nor am I saying there was no struggle in his little mind, but he did it! And he did it out of love for his family. That's the point I'm trying to make.

God wants us to give out of sacrificial love in order to demonstrate to all that He's the one we love the most! Most of us at this point in reading a book or listening to a sermon scramble our brains and say, "Okay, now tell me how to do it. Give me details, step by step." We are over-achievers! We've learned and have been trained to get it right, get it done!

Nope, I'm not going to do it, at least not in full. You see I want you to find out in practical, personal details what is pleasing to the one you love the most. I've been working on that in my life for years. My relationship with Christ is everything to me. So I've been on my own personal journey of giving the gift of obedience to my King. I want to wrap it up, make it beautiful and deliver it daily from my heart to His.

Yes, I've been coached along the way, just like Gandalf coached Bilbo Baggins to stay on the path. I've listened to sermons, I've been in Bible studies, I've been discipled, mentored and more. I've read the Puritans, the old dead guys and even some of the new. I'm very thankful for those who have loved me and helped me on my journey. You may not know many, or any, of the old dead guys, but you should. They've pushed me to think Biblically as I've looked for the perfect gift for my God. As a result of their challenges to me, there have been no moments that satisfy me more, than when through my searching, investigating and digging in God's Word I discover the details of what pleases my LORD. It's the best! You see, I've personally done the work and it's from my heart to His.

This loving gift of obedience can be expressed in so many ways as we live each day for the glory of our God. And as we search the Scriptures for the details and particulars of what He loves to get from us, it should create excitement in our hearts because it pleases our God. That's what Paul told us to do in Ephesians—find out what is pleasing to God. By the way, until I leave this earth to be in the presence of the One who has lived keeping the law for me, died and took the punishment of His Father for me and rose from the grave conquering all for me, I'll still be looking for that perfect piece of dark, dark chocolate.

POINTS to PONDER

1. Loving obedience is at the storm center of Jesus' words in Luke 14:25-33.
2. Transformation from spiritual death to spiritual life is proved by obedience. Do you agree or disagree? Explain your answer this time to God.
3. What would be some personal gifts you could give daily to your KING?
4. Subjective thinking is absolutely destructive in the area of obedience. Do you agree or disagree? Explain your answer to yourself and God.
5. Read Jesus' words again in John 14 and write them out in your own words.
6. There is no excuse for not pursuing this gift of obedience for God. If you do not, are you a true disciple of Jesus according to Luke 14?
7. Where do we find the definitions of true love and obedience?

IT IS THE TASK OF THE VISIBLE CHURCH
TO MAKE THE INVISIBLE REIGN OF CHRIST
VISIBLE TO THE WHOLE WORLD.
JOHN CALVIN

7

BLABBER MOUTHS

Isn't it correct to say something like Calvin did about the Great Commission found in Matthew chapter 28? Jesus told the boys He'd been training for three years, "Go, blab my story to the whole world. Go on and talk about Me, teach My doctrines and tell the whole world I've risen!" I know you're asking, "Where's the depth?" But, He really did say something like that. I think His point was to go and make more disciples. It may have sounded something like this, "Go with energy, joy and uncompromising loyalty to My cause and Kingdom. Teach all I've taught and commanded you! Love, serve, sacrifice, help and preach the gospel to a lost and hurting world. You've had a life changing experience. Now, tell it, share it and be blabber mouths driven by love." C'mon, there's really nothing like a blabbermouth driven by love—God's love—is there?

I mentioned to you earlier in the Prologue that this book comes out of teaching Luke 14:25-33 for many,

many years. One such instance was at a training conference in the Chicago area. There were high school students from all over the country that were in attendance. It's always a lot of fun and energy when you get together with hundreds of teenagers. We had training seminars that occupied most of the morning and in the afternoon we'd hit the city with the gospel. It was during the summer months, and therefore it was Chicago hot and humid. You could smell the Chicago hot dogs all over the city.

I was asked to hang out with one of the groups for the afternoon and I wisely chose the beach tour. My mama didn't raise a complete idiot. We loaded up the buses and off to Lake Michigan we went in a state of steamy sweat. If you've never been on a bus packed with students, you're missing a great adventure filled with surprises. We arrived at the lake where it was very pleasant and also jammed with humanity every place you looked. Our loving task for the afternoon was to tell people on the beach about Jesus. You got it; we were to be gentle and caring blabber mouths. A group of students asked me if I'd go with them for the mission that was given to us, and I did. We all had our little gospel booklets and Bibles with us for our blanket evangelism on a beautiful Chicago day. Gathering in a small circle, we prayed together for our adventure and then launched into the sand with lots of positive anticipation. We were like a group of nomads heading from blanket to blanket trying to get the privilege to blab about our King.

It was really hot. My feet were smoking. Surprisingly enough, I don't think people wanted to deal with our presentation. I was convinced they'd all rather be in the water. And that sounded like a pretty good idea to me too. Fervently, we pressed on farther and farther down the beach getting constantly rejected by the people that were tanning their bodies. I asked one of the younger girls if she was ready to try to share her faith with a person of her own choice. The look on her face was one of sheer terror and anxiety. We didn't need a girl passing out on the beach, so I told her, "Be cool, be calm, and don't worry about it."

I spoke up and said to the group that I'd try to share with somebody while they prayed for the encounter. I identified my target and cautiously proceeded to get his attention. At first, he seemed to be slightly irritated with my interruption to his day, but then he began to listen politely to me. We talked for a few minutes together about Jesus and I finally realized it was time to end the conversation with him. The students that had been praying for me came running toward me to find out what had happened. I told them that he was polite, but not really interested in spiritual matters. I looked at my young friends and comrades on the beach and asked, "Who's next?"

The freshman girl who had seemed freaked by our mission spoke up and said, "I'll try." God really does work in mysterious ways. Again we all gathered to pray for her and the person God would lead her to share with on that hot beach. We finished praying and made our way slowly through the maze of beach blankets covered with mankind, as the aroma of sweat and suntan oil wafted through the air. We walked and walked and looked and looked for the person she'd feel comfortable engaging. Then she said to all of us, "Right over there, that's the one."

It was an older man that she probably saw as a

grandpa figure and therefore felt safe. She carefully approached his blanket and began speaking to him about her faith in Christ. We were all too far away to hear the entire conversation they were having, but it appeared to be going well. The man took the gospel booklet from her and said to her, "Thank you." With that she bolted back toward us almost out of control with excitement. Over and over, she told us that he had listened to her and even asked some questions about her beliefs. We asked her all together, "How did it end?" Absolutely filled with a joyful heart about her experience of sharing her faith and the gospel story she exclaimed, "He'll think about it and maybe even pray about it."

This little girl found the internal celebration of being a blabber mouth for Jesus. Suddenly, she turned to all of us and asked, "Who's next?" So down the beach we all went and it was still very, very hot. Before I could stop our new aggressive evangelist, she'd gotten the attention of a group of guys, and that could be real trouble. I did manage to pull her back from the boys who were now very interested in our little blabber mouth.

They'd been playing catch with a football and I thought I'd join in with them and build a quick relationship. These guys were a group from the inner city of Chicago and were very street-wise. I asked if I could perhaps throw them some passes with the football and they all looked at me with startled expressions. I had grown up in Chicago and told them I can throw the ball, hoping there was a connection. One of the guys tossed the ball to me and took off running expecting me to throw a pass to him. The ball was now in my hands, so I thought it was a personal challenge of some type. I launched the ball and prayed it would get to him or at least be close. It was a perfect spiral and he caught it on the run. The other guys were amazed that I'd thrown the ball that far and that it was a spiral. We'd connected over a football and continued to play together for a long time, in the heat of the day. What was I thinking?

The students I had been with patiently waited to see what would happen next. Finally, we stopped and I was really happy about that because of the heat. I then asked the guys if they'd all be willing to listen to a presentation from one of our students. They all began to sit down in the sand and motioned to go ahead and do it. You got it! Our little blabber mouth couldn't wait to share the gospel and she did it with boldness. Man, we were all proud of her at that moment. On a hot beach in front of all of those guys, she shared Jesus.

I don't really know the final outcome and that's what everybody always wants to know. Did that little girl give an altar call on the beach? Or, how many of those tough guys prayed to receive Christ? Did they all crawl forward together in the hot sand? We prayed together for all of those guys, but were there any of them who trusted in Christ at that precise moment? I don't know. But what I do know for sure is that the freshman girl who'd been scared to death was not ashamed to blab and do what Jesus called all of us to do in Luke 14 and Matthew 28: speak up about Him, and to never be ashamed to follow HIm. How could anyone in their right mind ever be ashamed of the ONE they loved the most?

Paul said in Romans 1, "For I am not ashamed of the gospel, for it is the power of God for salvation." Earlier in the chapter he says, and I paraphrase, "I've been set apart for the gospel. I will serve God with my spirit in the gospel. I'm eager to preach the gospel." Jesus had met

Paul on the road to Damascus while he was on his way to torture or to kill those who followed Jesus. He was lost, under the curse of the law and relentlessly committed to destroying this Jesus cult following. In my opinion, I believe he was convinced that it was his Pharisaical duty, and if it was accomplished, he'd be a national religious hero of some type.

But whatever we want to think about Paul doesn't really matter. What matters is what God's Word says about the situation. Paraphrased from Acts 9, here's what it says (but please take some time to read it on your own): Paul was standing in the direct path of God's wrath and if he continued on this course of rejecting Christ and His gospel, eternal punishment would be his end. But on that road of sovereign grace, he was made into a new creature in Christ. Instantaneously, supernaturally, he was rescued by the One he sought to destroy. In the snap of a finger, the clap of a hand, the blink of an eye or the beat of a heart, the grace of God invaded his life. The gospel exploded into his life and blew it up, giving him abundant life and a new, eternal purpose. The love, mercy and grace of God had given him the ability to understand the message of the gospel, and he'd be forever grateful and never ashamed. He may have become the loudest blabber mouth this world has ever heard besides Jesus.

When you comprehend the gospel, you can't help but tell somebody. When Linda and I had our first son... well, actually *she* had him... the experience was unbelievable. After Jonathan was born, and I knew both of them were alright for the evening, I left the hospital. I drove home down a very, very busy street in Chicago. My window was wide open and my emotions were exploding all over the place, and that can be messy. I was yelling out as loud as possible, "I'm a Daddy, I've had a baby." I don't remember the exact words I spewed out of my mouth, but they were something like that. People looked at me as if they were looking at a madman. I was! My life had been invaded by a little boy and I would never be the same again. The moment was powerful and there was big life change on the way for me. I was introduced to cloth diapers and wake-up calls in the middle of the night. The wake-up calls weren't too bad; it was the cloth diapers that were painful at times. And for those of you who have never had the pleasure of using them, you should find a way! You used pins the size of darning needles to keep them on the baby. My fingers were full of holes from those stinkers. They hurt!

Our new little boy brought incredible life change for all of us and there was no shame. A life had been given by God and I was not ashamed. Remember the story I told you earlier about Linda and me? When she finally agreed to be my girl—do you think I was ashamed? Are you kidding me? I think I head-butted every locker in the locker room, and that's why I have issues with my brain, as you can tell. The pain in my head didn't matter because she was mine and everyone in our school needed to know. I was a BLABBER MOUTH of the most amazing kind.

When I was a youth pastor, one of my mentors taught me, "Christ didn't save us to be secret agents." And just like I was not about to keep it a secret concerning Linda, we're not to be silent about our relationship with Christ. Listen to Jesus' own words about the silent or "secret agent" attitude. In Matthew 10:32-33, He says, "So everyone who acknowledges Me before men, I will also acknowledge before My Father who is in heaven, but whoever denies Me before men, I also will deny before my Father who is in heaven." I'm thinking He's very serious about this public identification with Him! Why? Read on and you'll see what I mean.

In Luke 12:8-9, He says it a bit differently, but He says it. "And I tell you, everyone who acknowledges me before men, the Son of Man also will acknowledge before the angels of God, but the one who denies me before men will be denied before the angels of God." Jesus communicates clearly to everyone that there must be no secret religious agents in His community. Did you notice I added the word, *religious*? Believe me, you can be loaded with religion and have no true relationship with Jesus. I'm not sure I can concisely explain the whole mystery of the secret agent puzzle, but that's the point. What you need to think about is that when you're a secret agent, nobody knows who you really are, perhaps not even yourself. That's a scary thought.

I have a question for you that I want you to think about in all sincerity. Is it possible to think that you're saved when you're really not saved? Sounds crazy, doesn't it? I promise you this challenge comes from a heart of love and concern. I've seen way too many individuals professing a relationship with Christ within the local church setting. But outside of the church their mouths are closed. Their lifestyles also deny that they have become new creatures in Christ. But, based on their own opinions, they're convinced.

I'm going to paraphrase here, but I want you to read the text in Matthew 7:15-23. He told the people hanging out with Him, "You'll know a tree by its fruit—good or bad. People will say to Him, 'Lord, Lord we're yours.' His response will be to say to them, 'Depart from me I never knew you.'" Please take time and read it, even right now.

> Matthew 7:15-23 English Standard Version (ESV)
> 15 "Beware of false prophets, who come to you in sheep's clothing but inwardly are ravenous wolves. 16 You will recognize them by their fruits. Are grapes gathered from thornbushes, or figs from thistles? 17 So, every healthy tree bears good fruit, but the diseased tree bears bad fruit. 18 A healthy tree cannot bear bad fruit, nor can a diseased tree bear good fruit. 19 Every tree that does not bear good fruit is cut down and thrown into the fire. 20 Thus you will recognize them by their fruits. 21 "Not everyone who says to me, 'Lord, Lord,' will enter the kingdom of heaven, but the one who does the will of my Father who is in heaven. 22 On that day many will say to me, 'Lord, Lord, did we not prophesy in your name, and cast out demons in your name, and do many mighty works in your name?' 23 And then will I declare to them, 'I never knew you; depart from me, you workers of lawlessness.'

Jesus told the crowds all through His earthly ministry in various ways what I've been babbling about, "I saved you to be my witnesses to a lost, condemned world." We get our English word, "witness" from the original language that the New Testament is written in. The word is "martyr" and to be a martyr was to be persecuted for your life message. The Christian's life message is the gospel. We're to tell His story and live the life He has called us to, with love in the face of everyone we meet.

A TRUE DISCIPLE OF CHRIST MAY FAIL FOR THE MOMENT, BUT THE PATTERN OF HIS OR HER LIFE WILL BE OPEN IDENTIFICATION WITH THE DEMANDS OF JESUS WITHOUT SHAME.

If you're not sure what spontaneous combustion is, Google it. I believe God's work in us causes us to be spontaneously combustible. That is, we can't control our loving, intelligent, emotional outbursts about our relationship with Jesus. We've gotta blab! We're compelled by love for Him. He told the believers in 1 Peter 2:9-10, "But you are a chosen race, a royal priesthood, a holy nation, a people for His own possession, that you may proclaim the excellencies of Him who called you out of darkness into His marvelous light." No secret agents, but instead a group of people delivered from darkness and driven by love to be blabber mouths. We are to actively blab and proclaim the amazing work of God's grace in our lives.

Peter was encouraging the Christians he was writing to blab the gospel even though Nero was persecuting them. They were fed to lions, tarred and stuck on poles to be set on fire as human torches in Nero's garden. They were butchered for his sick pleasure. But Peter told them to live, love, and tell the story of Jesus. Love the people that were killing them by telling them about the gospel of hope and peace.

None of us are perfect—that's for heaven. But I think as Peter wrote, he must have remembered: "I failed Him, I cursed Him, I denied Him and He still forgave and is using me." If you're like Peter and me, you've failed to blab on occasion. Maybe you've been concerned about how it might impact your life's situation? Press on! He's called us to work out our salvation with fear and trembling. So work it out! Do what Christ said without being a religious fake. A true disciple of Christ may fail for the moment, but the pattern of his or her life will be open identification with the demands of Jesus without shame! That's at the heart of being a blabber mouth.

My dad, who is now hanging out in heaven with his Savior, always ended his notes to me in this way, "Keep on Keepin' On." So, keep on! Don't worry about people and what they think. When I was hanging out my car window driving down that busy street in Chicago, I didn't care what people were thinking. I'd been given a great gift—a little baby. He was my little buddy and I was his daddy. We had a precious relationship given by God, and I wanted the whole world to know about it! So, go on, speak, brag, boast, shout and blab about the One that you love the most. Find your own street and do a little spontaneous combustion for Jesus, while making sure you get the gospel right.

POINTS to PONDER

1. All true believers will be blabber mouths for Jesus. Do you agree or disagree?
2. Why do we struggle with blabbing about Jesus and living for Him with a blabbing lifestyle?
3. The Church has been infiltrated by secret agents who damage the church community's reputation. Do you agree or disagree? If you agree, what action, if any, should be taken?
4. What can you personally do to become a more effective blabber mouth?

I'LL SPEAK OF HIM WHO DIED FOR ME,
I'LL SPEAK OF HIM WHO SET ME FREE,
HE GAVE AND GAVE THAT I MIGHT BE
A LOVING LIFE FOR ALL TO SEE.
MY MOUTH I'LL OPEN WIDE AND TELL ABOUT THIS HERO KING,
WHO CAME TO EARTH TO LIVE FOR ME ABOUT HIM I WILL SING

AUTHOR UNKNOWN
(But a member of the Blabber Mouth Club)

IF WHAT YOU CALL YOUR FAITH IN CHRIST DOES NOT INVOLVE
TAKING THE SLIGHTEST NOTICE OF WHAT HE SAYS-THEN IT IS NOT
FAITH AT ALL-NOT FAITH OR TRUST IN HIM, ONLY INTELLECTUAL
ACCEPTANCE OF SOME THEORY ABOUT HIM.

C.S. LEWIS

THE FIRST DEMAND WHICH IS MADE OF GOD'S CHURCH IS THAT
THEY SHALL BE WITNESSES OF JESUS CHRIST BEFORE THE WORLD.

DIETRICH BONHOEFFER

8
BLOOD FOR BLOOD

Wow, we've gone from blabber mouths to blood for blood, which sounds like an etymological train wreck, or a bad movie. What are these crazy words doing in this book, especially "blood for blood"? I'm not certain I'll be able to explain all I'm thinking about or trying to communicate, but I'll try.

First of all, the Bible is loaded with all kinds of bloody stories. So that's one good reason to talk about blood—I mean it! If you took some of those stories and made movies with them, it would almost be too much for our minds to process. Hollywood would go crazy with them. Some people would get bent out of shape by all of it and for others, it might not even faze them. We all tend to be very subjective and opinionated people and have no problem expressing our feelings about most anything.

Linda was teaching a Sunday school class several years ago and telling the story of Jesus' crucifixion. It's a pretty bloody story, if you think Biblically about that momentous event. Linda is a great storyteller and is not gory or gross, like her husband can be. She has always been sensitive to families and their unique behavioral patterns and desires. But one of the students' parents, along with the child, was not happy with the story. In fact, they were offended by the blood scenes. They were a nice family, but Jesus had bled and died, and it was offensive to them. I'd better stop there, if you know what I mean. You can't escape the fact about our faith being a bloody one—it just is.

One of my favorite stories, and maybe yours too, is the Passover. The whole story is a bloody mess. Moses had shown up on the scene and was chosen by God to be the deliverer of His people, the Israelites. Pharaoh was a rascal, a problem, a reprobate. He was arrogant and prideful to the point where it would destroy him. Pride always has a way of accomplishing that in our lives. There was no way he'd let God get his slaves and kingdom-builders. He was warned over and over again, but in his blind ignorance and selfishness, he refused to change course. I want to make it clear at this point in the story that he was accountable for his sinful behavior. You know the rest of the story, right?

The plagues came and devastated the land. Go on and read the account in Exodus for yourself. I do have a favorite or two among the plagues. I like the frog festival and the bloody Nile River. I can just see Pharaoh trying to get those frogs out of his bed! And let's face it: no one is going to eat fish that has been swimming in blood for a few days. Sushi, anyone? But, it's the final plague that captivates my mind and powerfully grabs my heart. I might use some words here that you may need to look up in a Bible dictionary, but that's a good exercise for all of us. Let me list a few that would be good for you to investigate and meditate on for a while. So here's my short list: atonement, propitiation, expiation, sacrifice, substitution, Passover and redeemed. Redeemed—it's another precious word that describes one who is a Christ follower. Perhaps it should be the most important word in our lives as believers. Now, back to why I love the final plague.

Scripture talks about blood, guts (otherwise known as entrails) and it deals with death. But there is one more word that is incredibly important to the story. That word is *DELIVERANCE*! God would choose to deliver His people from the Angel of Death if they would be obedient and trust in His word. He gave them clear instructions on how to avoid His wrath and punishment. You need to read the instructions for yourself in the Old Testament book of Exodus, beginning in chapter 12. Read the entire chapter several times asking God to grant you a deeper understanding of His work of mercy and grace. I want to remind those who are squeamish that the chapter is filled with blood. I'm going to paraphrase that story and the instructions God gave in the next few words. Read my description carefully, and then read God's word with reverence. You should never give your complete trust to anyone's paraphrase.

Moses had been told by God to instruct the Israelites to take an unblemished lamb, one without any imperfections, and kill it. The lamb was to be offered as a perfect sacrifice to please God. They would kill it, bleed it and eventually eat all of it properly according to all of God's instructions. God is very clear with His demands for His people. Read the text. He wanted His people to understand how to live, and not die, as the Angel of Death came through the land. They were told to do exactly what He said. After the killing of the lamb, they were to take some of the blood and put it on the two doorposts and lintel of the house in which they ate of the lamb. The families were then to go inside the house, and with the blood of the lamb on their front door, the Angel of Death would pass over them, delivering them from death. Kill the perfect lamb, get the blood on the door and get under the blood, and be delivered from God's wrath. That is what they were told by God to do in order to live and be delivered.

I love this bloody, sacrificial story. I love it, love it, love it, because it is the powerful picture of Jesus as the perfect sacrificial Lamb of God who came to take away the sin of the world! He did what Adam failed to do for our human race. Jesus kept the law when tempted by the devil, as He was battling for our souls. He substituted Himself in the place of those who would believe in Him. He took their sin in His body and experienced the physical, emotional, and eternal wrath of His Father. Most people get caught up in the physical crucifixion of Christ and miss the great supernatural doctrine that He actually experienced hell. You may struggle with this doctrinal issue, but I'm asking you to think about it. This is the great mystery of Divine Providence. He arose from the grave, conquering death and all evil for His people! He sacrificed, He bled and He alone saves by faith those who get under His HOLY, ROYAL BLOOD.

If you're not getting the connection to the story in Exodus, please continue to think about it. Hopefully, I haven't confused you. Jesus is my Passover Lamb and I pray that He's yours. I had to work through this with you as the reader in order for you to understand the Blood for blood title of this chapter. Our faith is really centered on this teaching. The Christian life is a mix of celebration, commitment, pain, peace and blood. This is app #4 of the theme, "You'll do anything for the one you love the most." I'm convinced that we'll do anything, or make any sacrifice for the one we love the most. The person or possession that has our highest affections in this life gets all of us! Jesus offered Himself willingly, labored in Himself willingly, and poured out Himself willingly unto death. He didn't do it hoping that His substitutionary sacrifice on the cross might save somebody. He wrote the script. His people would be saved from their sins. He did what no human being could ever do or will ever do. And so, app #4 is this: He calls us to respond out of love for Him and live lives of holy sacrifice.

That can be painful, perhaps even bloody. But, let's face it—if you're in your right mind, you don't crave pain. If you're in your right mind, right? So what was Jesus doing? Was He out of His mind? No, He had full understanding of His mission. He offered Himself freely and took incomprehensible pain for those He would save. In the same way, we're to offer ourselves, understanding that we'll never experience the same type of pain He did. But, there will be pain.

I played football for six years, and there was plenty of bloody pain. So why did I play football? Why did I offer my body on the field of athletic competition and sacrifice? Because I enjoyed pain? No, I didn't crave pain or spilling my blood on the 50-yard line. I didn't stand out there and scream, "Hit me" over and over again like an idiot. But, as you probably know, even if you've never played, the game of football is full of pain at any level. When I played pee-wee football, I broke a kids arm and put a nail through my hand. The kid whose arm I broke laid there writhing in excruciating pain. But I played on even after seeing all of that pain. In high school, the pain levels increased. I mean they really got intense. I saw blood and more blood, and even some guts on occasion.

In my ninth-grade year of high school, I weighed 120 pounds at best. We had guys on the varsity team that weighed upwards of 275 pounds and were 6'7" or 6"8", or it seemed that way to a little guy like me. They were monsters to me and monsters are scary. They can break you into itsy, bitsy pieces. During one of my first practices with the varsity squad, a monster pressed his spikes into my chest leaving a monster-size shoe tattoo in the middle of my tiny pectorals. He looked at me just like monsters do and said, "Welcome to the team, you little punk." I didn't cry or say anything to him that might make things any worse for me. I loved the game of football and was willing to take all the abuse to my body that went with it! I loved football so much that I'd carry a ball around with me during school. And hopefully without sounding too strange, I loved to sleep with that little pigskin. I even loved the smell of that little piggy.

Sometimes during our practices there was a drill we used to do called Lovers' Lane. I promise you, it is not what you think at all. It terrified most all of us small dudes. The coach would take blocking dummies and make a lane with them. The massive linemen and linebackers would stand at one end of the lane by him, and the running backs and the rest of us at the opposite end facing them. He'd also lay some dummies across the lane that you would have to jump over. When the whistle blew, if you were in the front of the line, it was your turn to get loved at the other end of the lane.

It's not always easy to remember all the names of the guys on our team, but there was one you'd never forget. His name alone was frightening besides the size of his big monster body. He was huge. I'm not going to mention his name—let's just call him Monster—just in case he gets his hands on this read and comes looking for me. I stood in line and waited for the sound of the whistle and prayed, "Please not Monster!" My first or second practice I stood waiting and hoping it wouldn't be him. I kept my head down and my fear concealed and waited in the heat of the afternoon. As I got closer to the front of the line I quickly peeked and counted to see who was waiting to give me some love. On the inside, my stomach knotted and my heart palpitated. If my calculations were correct, it was him—THE MONSTER! I started telling myself, "You can do this. No fear, no fear. You can do this."

It was my turn there in the front of the line of doom and possible death. The whistle was headed toward the coach's mouth and if I was going to bail, now was the time to do it! Walk away, make an excuse, puke, do something to get out of this painful situation. Think about it for a minute. Why in the world would anybody in their right mind do this, making this sacrifice of body and soul and perhaps even some brain matter? I knew the pain was waiting for me at the other end of that lane.

I heard the sound of the whistle, ran down Lovers' Lane and then felt the initial blow of The Monster! As I came to my senses, I was crawling on my knees with tears coming down my cheeks in absolute silence. My brain was ringing and the pain I felt was intense. I felt like

Quasimodo, the hunchback of Notre Dame, who had just had a bad bell experience. But, I absolutely loved football and there was no sacrifice that I was unwilling to make for that little piggy. Believe it or not, all 120 pounds of me made my way to the back of the line and waited for my next turn. And, believe it or not, I got the Monster again. The whistle blew and it was déjà vu. I ran and caught the football, then nearly vaporized by the impact.

Why do we do these things? I really had an almost foolish love for the game of football. I got hit so hard during a game my senior year, that I walked off the field toward Linda (who was a cheerleader) and yelled out, "I love you!!!" The coach grabbed me and shoved some of that stinky stuff up my nose and I was back in the game. I loved it!! I had broken fingers, broken ribs, an injured neck, bruises, and raspberries that were massive and painful. But I loved the game and I'd make almost any sacrifice for the privilege of playing it.

Football could never save me from eternal punishment. But I would bleed for it over and over again. I hope you're making the connection with Christ's call to those of us who say that we're Christians. In Luke 14:25-33, His demand is clear. Those He would sacrifice and bleed for must, in return, sacrifice and bleed for Him. It sounds all too demanding of Jesus, doesn't it? But if you really consider it, how demanding was it for Him to take hell for those who'd believe? He told the crowds to think. He never enticed, deceived, or manipulated them. He also used beautiful teaching illustrations to make it clear. He told them the world would mock those who started to follow Him, but didn't finish. Jesus never looked for a jump-on-the-bandwagon response. He challenged the thought-process and never misled the people. He told them, "This is my offer." He was the Messiah and would do the supernatural work. If they came to Him, they'd never thirst again. If they believed in Him, they wouldn't be guilty for their sin and they'd be free from the curse of the law. If they came to Him, His yoke was easy and the burden light. But He demanded in return, a life of perhaps painful sacrifice and uncompromising allegiance to His commands.

If you Google the word "sacrifice," it will probably be different than the original 1828 Webster's definition. It's really pretty amazing to me that Webster began by defining the word in Biblical terms: "Sacrifice is to offer to God in homage or worship, by killing and consuming as victims on an altar." I've never had the privilege to speak with Mr. Webster, but I believe I will someday.

At the root meaning of the word, sacrifice is blood and pain. He makes a direct connection to animal sacrifice in the Old Testament. He was very aware of the Biblical patterns of pleasing God in worship by offering a victim for slaughter on His altar.

INTERNAL CHANGE BY GOD PRODUCES EXTERNAL CHANGE FOR GOD.

In the New Testament epistle of Romans, Paul also makes a clear connection with Old Testament altar sacrifice. After he's explained to his readers all that God's done for those who had been declared not guilty by faith in the works of Christ, he begins to tell them what God now demands from them. If you can remember, it almost sounds like my interaction with the girls at the bowling alley in chapter 1. I explained God's grace, and that His grace changes our lives. You need to read Paul's words for yourself, but he says something like this, "Let your life be a living holy sacrifice, let the world be your altar, crawl up on it, live and die for Christ. Let them see your blood spilled out of love for Him." That's my paraphrase. He finishes with something like this, "It's your spiritual worship. God deserves it. It's reasonable and you owe HIM!"

These words of Paul are almost too difficult to comprehend, let alone live daily. His words are frightening, because sacrifices always died. And without any apologies, he was telling them to actively pursue their own death. To his readers, he's written a letter of love. Paul wanted the followers of Christ to be motivated internally and not manipulated by his powerful personality. I referred to it earlier in this chapter—that internal change by God produces external change for God.

I'd never teach that the sacrifices we make for Jesus save us from His Father's wrath. But I want you to think hard about this. When Paul, the former killer of Christians understood the love, mercy and grace of God that delivered him from the eternal punishment of the Holy Godhead, he was personally overcome with adoration and gratitude. As a result of his understanding he would live and teach all of us to spill our blood for Christ. I believe that's why he ends Romans 11 with this:

Romans 11:33-35 English Standard Version (ESV)
33 Oh, the depth of the riches and wisdom and knowledge of God! How unsearchable are his judgments and how inscrutable his ways! 34 "For who

has known the mind of the Lord, or who has been his counselor?" 35 "Or who has given a gift to him that he might be repaid?" 36 For from him and through him and to him are all things. To him be glory forever. Amen.

It was an outburst of overflowing gratitude to God. Paul was a transformed, regenerated, Spirit-changed man and there was no sacrifice he was unwilling to make for Jesus. If you don't understand all of those words, it's your responsibility to discover what they mean. They should be precious to those who profess to be a Christ-follower.

I want to be careful here, but if there's no grasp at all about what you've just read, something's not right in your life. Paul was changed by God's grace and was driven to sacrifice and bleed for the One he loved the most. I'm sure he went through many soul searching nights. Paul, perfect in Christ, was still a man that battled with the flesh and all its ugliness. Pouring out his life as a drink offering in the service of his King, he was finally beheaded by Nero outside of Rome. Paul understood and willingly and lovingly made the ultimate sacrifice for His King. I believe the motto of his life is one that most of us know and applaud. It's found in his letter to the Philippians in 1:20-21, "as it is my eager expectation and hope that I will not be at all ashamed, but that with full courage now as always Christ will be honored in my body, whether by life or death. For to me to live is Christ and to die is gain."

In John MacArthur's commentary on the Gospel of Matthew, he tells an amazing story about a little boy named Yusufu. It's another story of God's transforming grace and it's powerful. But then again, as Romans states clearly, the "gospel is the *power* of God unto salvation." The gospel exploded into this young African boy's life and rearranged everything. The one he loved the most would now be Christ. And like the apostle Paul or anyone understanding what Jesus did for them, he offered his life on the altar of sacrifice. He refused to be ashamed of Christ when asked to renounce Him. He refused to submit to the king's authority and continued to obey the Word of God. He was threatened over and over again. They told him he'd be burned alive if he persisted in his new belief.

Every time I read or tell his story, I'm overcome with emotion because of this boy's commitment to Jesus. He was taken to be burned alive and when they went to tie him to the stake, he said, "Don't cut my arms off for I will not run from the flames that carry me to my Lord." It wasn't just a threat to scare a little kid. It wasn't tribal scare tactics to break his will to follow his new King. The king and his warriors were dead serious. They would share no loyalty to any other leader, so they burned him alive.

So why does it stir my emotions, ripping and squeezing at my heart? It's because I want to be as courageous for my King as he was. I want to live and not fear the powers of this temporal world. This story, like so many others that we've heard or read about, challenges our faith. It's the apostle Paul's motto on steroids and more. We sometimes love the stories of the martyred as they can have a weird romantic effect on us at times. At other times, when our affections are captivated by the world and the things in it, we'd rather not listen to them. But we've got to evaluate and ask ourselves, why? Why is it that sometimes we love them and at other times we almost hate to hear them told? It's the responsibility of each of us who say that Jesus is the One we love the most to consider these tough issues.

He's called us to a Blood for blood relationship with Him and wouldn't it be incredible for the world to see the bride of Christ living this way? Wouldn't it be amazing for them to see that we're not just a bunch of crazy, religious, condemning, and pious people who go to a church building on the weekend, making the claim that we're different than they are. The problem is obvious to them as they observe our lives during the week. We make great sacrifice for the same things they do. We share many of the same idols and bump into them as we meet at the many altars of the world's gods. Their observation leads them to the conclusion that we're just like them. We covet, desire, work and live for all of the same things that they do. We're just seen by them as a strange little religious group that's not any different. We just gather together on Sundays.

The word *different* needs to be understood, because that's exactly what we're commanded to be. Our lives and everything about us must be offered on the altar of holy sacrifice daily being absolutely surrendered to Jesus. It would have to impact somebody. A bloody mess always gets our attention. Think about that for a moment before you read on.

In the little book titled *Gems from Tozer*, A.W. Tozer writes, "A whole new generation of Christians has come up believing that it is possible to "accept" Christ without forsaking the world. To accept Christ it is necessary that we reject whatever is contrary to Him. To "Accept Christ" is to know the meaning of the words 'as He is, so we are in this world.' (1 John 4:17) We accept His friends as our friends, His enemies as our enemies, His ways as our ways, His rejection as our rejection, His cross as our cross, His life as our life and His future as our future."

Whenever I quote someone, I realize it's not the easiest thing to understand. Sometimes when I'm out speaking somebody will ask me what the quote means. Who said it, or what was the reason I used it? You've got this one right in front of you, and it's a good one. A.W. Tozer was one of the most powerful Bible teachers in the 1950's and early 1960's. God used him to shake, rattle, rock and roll the churches during those years all across our country. He was asked to speak at the most popular conferences. He was loved and aggressively sought after by many denominations until he began confronting them because of their appetite for worldly entertainment instead of truth.

He was good friends with a pastor in England, who was also used by God to shake it up. Tozer wrote his friend a letter toward the end of his life telling him his popularity in conference speaking was diminishing rapidly. In fact, he said it this way, "I've preached my way off of every conference platform in America!"

I've read almost all of his published works. And I've also had the privilege to interact with one of his biographers for an entire afternoon. I love and admire A.W. Tozer. We could benefit from his powerful Biblical teaching today. But I know why his popularity began to decrease. He simply refused to be influenced by the world's influence on the local church. The church had lost its focus and the gospel was being diluted and watered down. The message of Christ in Luke 14:25-33 and other similar texts was being forgotten or taught incorrectly. He was viewed as an out-of-touch, old-fashioned prophet

GOD'S GRACE CHANGES A PERSON AND THAT CHANGE IS SEEN IN A SACRIFICIAL LIFESTYLE.

who didn't have the entertaining skills of the new kids on the block. He relentlessly but lovingly called the believers of his day to a life of individual holiness and sacrificial living. The Blood for blood commitment was a priority in his life and teaching. They didn't enjoy that and his platform appearances became less, less and less. He was a man in "Pursuit of God."

I've included this little touch of Tozer to entice you to become friends with him through his books. I'm very grateful for his impact in my life even though we don't agree on everything doctrinally. But we do agree on this: God's grace changes a person and that change is seen in a sacrificial lifestyle. It's not a lifestyle of perfection, but it is one set on daily surrender to their Lord. A *BLOOD* relationship that's lived out daily, second by second, minute by minute, hour by hour, day by day, week by week, month by month and year by year until heaven. Meanwhile, isn't it amazing what we'll do for things like football? Think about it.

POINTS to PONDER

1. Christ demands a "Blood for blood" lifestyle from us!
2. The old hymn says, "Living for Jesus a life that is true; striving to please Him in all that I do." Think about it and explain it in your own words.
3. Is it impossible to live a life of sacrifice for Christ in today's society?
4. Is Christ's call to a sacrificial life only for mature disciples?
5. Most of us are compromisers in some way and don't know what to do about it. Do you agree or disagree? Explain it to yourself out loud.
6. An old dead guy named Martin Luther said, "We will always do what we really want to do." Was he right?

TO KNOW CHRIST IS THE SUM AND THE ESSENCE
OF THE CHRISTIAN LIFE.
ALBERT BARNES

9
PLAY TIME

I want to begin this chapter and the end of this book with a statement I've come to love: *a relationship always produces a response*! I'm convinced that statement is absolute fact. Remember you've got the right to disagree, but I think I'm right in this instance. If you like or love someone, there's always a response in some way. The response may be words, hugs, money given, or even kisses! And if you dislike someone, or have even nasty feelings towards them, there's a response of another type. The reality of this response can be incredibly ugly and vulgar. If you're indifferent towards somebody, there's yet another response. No response! Expressed in some other words that are similar to our first statement, we might say a relationship causes a reaction of some magnitude. It always will.

I was speaking at an event and a friend told me this story about two families that shared a special relationship. Apparently, the families had gone on a little trip together and stopped at a large state park. Each family had one high school-aged son who were very good friends. They took off exploring the park together and eventually got separated from each other. What do you think? I think they're in high school and having some fun like buddies always do!

Finally, after quite a while, one of the guys needed to, in a word, use the facilities. He ran in to the rustic bathroom and suddenly realized that there was someone ahead of him in the stall. Isn't that a strange name for a bathroom? To me it sounds like a place for horses. Sorry, my mind wanders. The kid who was waiting now noticed the large shoes sticking out from under the door of that little stall and they were identical to his friends. His eyes widened as he realized it was his friend—at least he thought it was. Remember, this is a story about two buddies in their teens that have a relationship, which I believe always produces a response of some type.

Staring at the shoes he whispered, "Somebody is really smelling up this place." He was obviously playing around and trying to freak out his friend, but there was no response. So he said it louder and there was still no response. He moved closer and shouted it louder, with no reaction from the stall. Frustrated that his friend was not playing the game, he took drastic measures to get a response from him. He laid his back down on the gross bathroom floor and grabbed the door with his hands. With one swift motion, he slid under the door. With his head now under the door between the shoes, he was looking up into the face of somebody he'd never seen before in his life! I've told that story many times and people laugh and some others just look at me weird. That story is crazy! If I would have been in the stall, I might have had a heart attack. Hopefully I wouldn't have stomped on somebody's face. Now that would have been a reaction, but probably not the one to help us understand what we're talking about here. If I had been the man in the stall, I might never use a public restroom again—at least not a bathroom in a state park.

So, what's the point? No relationship, no response! The guy in the stall didn't respond. He was probably in a state of shock. He clearly didn't recognize the voice he'd heard making those goofy remarks. There was no relationship and a relationship always produces a response. Jesus said in John 10, and I paraphrase, "My sheep hear my voice and follow me." They respond because there's an intimate relationship with their Shepherd. He knows them and they know Him. I have this crazy picture in my head of the little fur balls jumping up and heading His way. Some are faster than others, but they're all up and moving toward their Shepherd's loving voice. Jesus might have to do a little goading, and we may get some strange grunts from the sheep, but they respond because of the intimate relationship with Him.

A living, loving, intimate relationship with Jesus is what this book is all about. I've expressed that idea in a lot of ways, but that's the main thought. The book began with a story about two girls and a bunch of students in a bowling alley. If you remember, one of the girls said, "My friend prayed the prayer asking Jesus into her heart." And like so many others, she was convinced she'd done what was required of her to go to heaven. When I challenged her with the words of Jesus in Luke 14:25-33, she walked away like so many others have, and still do. The demand of giving all to Christ was not what she had understood.

I'm convinced that many today are being taught,

listening to and believing in a false gospel. I've heard things that would be comparable to *The Wizard of Oz's* Dorothy clicking her heels three times together to go home to Kansas. Some of you might be thinking, "But Chuck, you were the speaker, you gave the gospel that night, right?" I did, but it would never have been a man-centered gospel. It wasn't filled with clichés, manipulation, and easy-believism doctrine. The content would never have focused on what man thinks he can do to save himself, instead only on what Christ had done. It would have concluded with a challenge to repent and believe in Jesus and His works!

Through the years, I've learned that people will change what they've heard in order to feel comfortable and secure with their eternal destiny. They convince themselves in their minds that their opinions and feelings about the gospel are truth. People have told me what they think I've said when it's never been in my head or come out of my mouth. It's a terrifying experience to be a teacher, especially one trying to represent God and His Word. It's almost as if people think I've made the gospel too complex. So they try to fix my mess. They're convinced I've got it wrong.

I'm not alone. There's a whole group of us that are getting "fixed" all the time when it comes to the gospel. Someone once said that people hear what they want to hear and disregard the rest. That issue of disregarding the rest is an important part of communicating truth in the church today. I believe God is raising up a group of young men in particular that are leading the charge of explaining the gospel Biblically. The gospel centers on repentance and faith in the works of Christ alone, and nothing else! It also produces a lifestyle of loving obedience.

Sadly, the girl in the bowling alley was misled by a well-intentioned friend, and I tried to correct the lie using God's Word. I lovingly explained the gospel and I took my time because her eternal destiny was at stake. She wanted heaven for a bargain, but didn't want to pick up her cross and follow. An old preacher named Vance Havner had this to say about the cross, "The marks of the cross are simply the marks of our identification with our Lord, death to our own plans and purposes, death to our own right to our lives, that He might have His way with us and ours." He also said, "What our Lord said about cross-bearing is not in fine type. It is in bold print on the face of the contract."

I've had people say to me this cross stuff and those demands in Luke 14 are for the advanced disciples and I should just share the entry-level gospel. You know, a Gospel 101. The thinking is that we should get the decision for Christ now, and then later on give them the demands of Jesus. Maybe we should red-shirt these people and give them an extra year in "The College of the Gospel". That approach sounds, to me, like a deceptive sales job, and happens all the time. It is the pressuring of individuals to "pray the prayer" and "ask Jesus into their heart." This form of what we call the gospel is destructive.

The gospel is the transforming work of the Spirit of God in our lives, beginning with grace and faith in Christ's works alone (salvation). It then leads us to a life that submits to His teaching (sanctification) and refusal of our subjective interpretations. When we use that kind of thinking and teaching, it only leads to emotional decisions which are false, and have the potential to destroy precious lives. More than ever before, we need concise, loving teaching of the gospel, whether it's inside or outside the church walls! It needs to be at the center of all of our discipleship and evangelism training. We need to get it right, and then patiently train camp counselors, Sunday School teachers, youth club leaders, youth staffers, small group leaders, everyone. I believe it honors God more than anything we can do as His people.

I told somebody not long ago that I was continuing to study and mine the treasures of the gospel. Wide-eyed, she responded by saying, "Don't you know that already? Why would you do that?" I shot back, in love, "I'm still learning. There's so much mystery in the gospel mines." The dwarves from *The Lord of the Rings* may have been on to something (I'm a digger). The understanding of the gospel is my number one goal, the priority of my life! I don't want to know it just to be a theological egghead, boasting in my disgusting flesh. I'm completely convinced that there's nothing else that pleases God more.

At the heart of the gospel, there beats a relationship with the infinite, eternal Godhead. I want to cultivate that relationship with all of my heart and mind! Think about that. You and I will never exhaust the mysteries of the *Mysterium Tremendum,* another term for God. The mysteries are there and waiting to be mined, dug, and enjoyed in the relationship we have with Him. And I'm convinced that our Heavenly Father loves it when His children come to Him saying, "Through Your Word teach me more. As your child I want to know more of who You are!"

When our grandson Travis was a little younger, he would crawl up on my lap and take those precious tiny fingers and squeeze my cheeks with all his might. Then he'd laugh (and he's got a great belly laugh). He'd look right into my eyes and say, "I love you Papa, play with me!" Over and over, he'd squeeze my face and say, "Play, play, play, Papa. Play with me." C'mon, you have to know I loved that moment in our relationship. It doesn't get a whole lot better than that. He's older now and he says it in a different way, but he still says it. "I love you, Papa. Let's play." We play together for hours— baseball, fishing, chess, hockey, horseback riding, reading. Can you see? We play, and we play hard!

Some of the jeans I wear have almost shredded off my body from our hours of playing together. I call them my "Travis Jeans". The jeans that aren't too badly destroyed I'll wear to camp. Students will ask me, "Where did you get those jeans? Are they expensive?" My answer is, "Yes." Then they ask, "How much?" I say, "A lot of love. These jeans represent a relationship of love that exists between my grandson and me and the many hours we've spent together playing on our knees."

A relationship always produces a response. My relationship with Travis continues to grow, and that's exactly what our Heavenly Father wants from us. He wants a relationship where, in our own way, we crawl up on His loving lap of compassion and wisdom and we say, "Play with me. Teach me." I know I've been repetitious with certain phrases or thoughts throughout the book. But someone has said repetition is the mother of all learning. So here's one of those phrases again: a relationship always produces a response. Do you hear that?

What will your response be to Christ's demands in Luke 14? At this point, how do you feel about the punches He's throwing your way? I've tried to give you some explanation and application of the text to chew on, along with stories of individuals who have aggressively lived out what Christ was teaching the crowds that hung around Him. I've given you some examples of living out His demands from our beautiful Christian heritage. They are people that some would see as going over and above what Jesus taught. But they really didn't. They simply met His demands, understanding it's a Blood for blood exchange, and they were willing to *do anything for the One they loved the most*. They wouldn't call themselves heroes, but we do, and perhaps, in a godly way, we should. Some of the names that flood my mind often are: Polycarp, Wycliffe, Savonarola, Huss, Peter Waldo, Zwingli, Luther, Calvin, Latimer, Ridley, Knox, Bunyan, Whitfield, Wesley, Edwards, Brainerd, Taylor, Carmichael, Mimosa, Spurgeon, Tozer, Jones, Elliot, Saint, Youderian, Fleming and McCully along with so many others that gave their all for Jesus.

We know the names of movie and television stars, musicians, singers, athletes, war heroes, authors and people on the covers of magazines. We invest our time in following and admiring their lives which will never be as profitable to us as studying the lives of the heroes of the faith. All of us need to dig up books on these individuals and others for the purpose of being mentored by them. Their relationship with Jesus was lived out in ways that we rarely see today. We need to study their lives and see how they personally worked at meeting Jesus' demands spelled out in Luke 14.

One of my personal favorites is a Puritan pastor named Thomas Watson. He lived during the days of the Separatist Movement in England. I won't take time to explain the battle that raged within the Church of

England, but he was in it and he left us several great books to read. Recently, I discovered one of them and it's knocked my socks off. The title of the book is *The Duty of Self Denial*. It's a powerful read that gives us more to consider about the demands of Jesus. Watson gives us some practical areas of life that we need to daily deny and surrender to Christ. Get the book. But for the time being, I'll give you a list to pray over and work on in your daily lives.

Some of us love to-do lists and some of us don't. So once again, let's call this a think-about list and leave it at that. The list comes directly from Watson himself. He was a true loving shepherd of his local church deeply caring for the souls of his people. I'm not going to explain all these points. I will simply ask you to prayerfully consider them.

1. A CHRISTIAN MUST DENY HIS REASON.
2. A CHRISTIAN MUST DENY HIS WILL.
3. A CHRISTIAN MUST DENY HIS OWN RIGHTEOUSNESS, HIS CIVILITIES, DUTIES AND GOOD WORKS.
4. A CHRISTIAN MUST DENY ALL SELF-CONFIDENCE.
5. A CHRISTIAN MUST DENY SELF-CONCEIT.
6. A CHRISTIAN MUST DENY HIS APPETITE. (EXCESS IN ALL THINGS)
7. A CHRISTIAN MUST DENY HIS EASE.
8. A CHRISTIAN MUST DENY CARNAL, WISDOM OF THE FLESH.
9. A CHRISTIAN MUST DENY HIS INORDINATE PASSIONS.
10. A CHRISTIAN MUST DENY HIS SINFUL FASHIONS.
11. A CHRISTIAN MUST DENY HIS OWN AIMS.
12. A CHRISTIAN MUST DENY ALL UNGODLINESS.
13. A CHRISTIAN MUST DENY HIS RELATIONS.

14. A CHRISTIAN MUST DENY HIS ESTATE FOR CHRIST.
15. A CHRISTIAN MUST DENY HIS LIFE FOR CHRIST.

I know. It's almost too much to digest, so don't pig out! Put it in the mind slowly and chew slowly! How many times are we told to chew our food before we swallow? I believe the same chewing process applies to brain food. It's great food! So take your time and digest it slowly—it honors God. Besides that, brain food ultimately comes from Him. It's the gospel lifestyle. It's Luke 14.

Thomas Watson was a Truth warrior. He battled for Truth until his last breath. His friends found him dead in his prayer closet. What a legacy to leave for all of us to meditate on and follow. I know, you're not sure you want to take off for heaven from a closet. But, what you should really remember about Watson is this: he would do anything for the One he loved the most. That's the message at the heart of this book and what should be at the center of our lives. For every true believer, it must be!

I was with a group of students, feeding some homeless people in Philadelphia. It was absolutely amazing how many showed up. They came from everywhere, two or three hundred, and more were coming all the time. We fed them soup and prayed for as many as possible with the time we had available to us. We all shared our faith in Christ up and down the street, with anyone who would listen. We were blabbing the best we could. I suddenly realized the group of men I was speaking to had drifted down the street and I was alone with them at the moment. We were having great conversations about Jesus, and how he loved people by caring for them and feeding them. Finally, I shared the gospel with them and their response was almost frightening. I hadn't been aware until that moment that they were primarily Muslims. They all seemed to be fine with Jesus until we got to His resurrection from the grave. To them, He'd been a good teacher and had died a type of martyr's death. But He was not God in the flesh. He was not God at all! The circle tightened as I continued to proclaim Him Lord of all and over all. I felt like I was in the middle of a boa-constrictor's grip and soon I'd be crushed to death. They pressed against my body and began to shove me a bit. I'd love to say to all of you reading this book that there was no fear in this tough guy's heart, but it was there. The commotion went on for a while and I thought, "I'm in trouble! Help!"

Some of the group I was with noticed something wasn't right, and came to my rescue. The circle opened and they pulled me out, and down the street we went. Thank God for youth leaders who help goofy guest speakers like me get out of tight jams. Sometimes when I think back on that event, I ask myself, "What were you doing?" My answers to that vary. They range from just being plain stupid to trying to impress the students and their leaders or perhaps fulfilling some crazy religious duty. Which one would you pick? And then there's at least one more. Maybe I was seriously trying to do it for the One I said I loved the most.

I'm really not sure what my motive was at that intense moment. But as I think back about Linda and our relationship, I know what my motive there was: I wanted a relationship with her, and I'd do anything to get it. When it came to playing football, I knew what my motive there was: I wanted to be quarterback and captain of the team, and I was willing to spill my blood to get it. Remember the monster?

My motives in those areas of life were clear. In the same way, I want my motives in serving Christ to be clear. I pray that your motives for serving Christ would be clear for you as well. Love is the motive. Because of His great love for me, I want to show my love for Him—the One I love the most—by being willing to do anything for Him. Hopefully, no person will ever take His place. Prayerfully, I'll be willing to openly identify with His cause and not run from persecution. And I want to eagerly sacrifice all my earthly possessions for His use. These are the three demands of Jesus we've considered throughout this book. They are the visible representation of God's grace—the gospel—that has worked, and is continuing to work, in our lives.

My prayer in the beginning for you was that you would be challenged in your thinking to consider the great call to true Biblical discipleship, grasp that character is more important than strategy, and clearly understand the gospel message. We all have a responsibility to seriously and prayerfully consider all these issues.

Martyn Lloyd-Jones, the great Welsh minister, made this statement about John Knox, who was a Scottish reformer: "Special men are needed for special times, and God always produces such men." I want you to know that I'll be praying for you, the reader, whether male or female, that God will produce in you a heart like John Knox. He had a heart that loved God's Word, loved God's people, and pleaded for the souls of the lost. His heart was one that would do anything for the One he loved the most.

Our times today are not much different than the times of John Knox. The battle for Truth and the gospel continues to rage, and special people are needed. Be one of those people. Thanks for taking time to read this book. I want you to know that I'm praying frequently for all those who will read and ponder these pages. I have one personal request of you: Please don't stick this book on the shelf as just another been-there-done-that reading project. We're all guilty of that. What I'm asking you to do is to continue to think about the truth you've read in this book and then pass it on to someone else who needs to hear this message.

My prayer is that your love for Jesus will increase and you'll submit to the demands of Luke 14. It proves that the gospel has saved you, transformed you and given you a new heart. This new heart clearly demonstrates to a lost and confused world your commitment to Jesus, the *ONE YOU LOVE THE MOST* and, the *ONE THEY NEED THE MOST*. So go on and do it for Him, motivated by His love for you. Anything, anything, anything!

MAKE ME THY FUEL, O' FLAME OF GOD.
AMY CARMICHAEL

MEDITATIONS FOR THE SOUL

I SOUGHT THE LORD AND AFTERWARD I KNEW,
HE MOVED MY SOUL TO SEEK HIM SEEKING ME.
IT WAS NOT I THAT FOUND NO SAVIOR TRUE, NO!
I WAS FOUND BY THEE.
AUTHOR UNKNOWN

MEN COME NOT TO CHRIST EXCEPT THROUGH THE WONDERFUL
AGENCY OF GOD. IT IS FIRST NECESSARY TO SHAKE THEM, THAT
THEY MAY UNLEARN THEIR WHOLE CHARACTER. OUR DISPOSITION
IS CHANGED AND WE RECEIVE THE YOKE OF CHRIST.
JOHN CALVIN

NO MAN CAN BE A TRUE CHRISTIAN WHO, WHEN HE MAKES A
PROFESSION, IS RESOLVED AFTER A WHILE TO TURN BACK TO THE
WORLD; NOR CAN HE BE A TRUE CHRISTIAN IF HE EXPECTS THAT HE
WILL TURN BACK.
ALBERT BARNES

TO THAT SOUL WHICH HAS TASTED OF CHRIST, THE JAUNTY
LAUGH, THE TEMPTING MUSIC OF MINGLED VOICES, THE
HAUNTING APPEAL OF SMILING EYES. ALL THESE LACK FLAVOR.
AND I WOULD DRINK DEEPLY OF HIM. FILL ME O' SPIRIT OF CHRIST
WITH ALL THE FULLNESS OF GOD.
JIM ELLIOT

TAKE MY LIFE AND LET IT BE....
(GO ON AND FINISH IT)
FRANCES HAVERGAL

ABOUT THE AUTHOR

Chuck Beckler is founder of True Direction Ministries and is passionate about seeing the gospel of Jesus Christ turn our world upside down. Chuck is a seasoned communicator and has been speaking to men, women, and students for more than 30 years. Neither just a lecturer nor an entertainer, Chuck communicates with sincerity to the hearts of people, not just to the heart of their problems. In addition to his ministry as a speaker and trainer, Chuck has served as a youth pastor and senior pastor in the suburbs of Chicago. He has maintained his credentials with the Evangelical Free Church of America since the mid-1980s. Chuck and his wife, Linda, currently reside in McHenry, IL.

For more information on True Direction Ministries or to see what the Becklers are up to today, please visit www.truedirectionministries.org.